The Dead See Everything

By

Glyn Lewis

This is a spine-chilling Psychological Thriller

Are you afraid?

You need to prepare.

Do you know what is awaiting you?

Have you seen the worst of Humanity?

Once you Enter the Gates, you may Never Get
Out.

Caution is key.

Be aware.

Someone is watching you.

When you think you are safe,

misguided.

Listen to the voices that you hear.

They are all 'Dead'.

The screams are Real.

The anguish is Real.

They are the ignored.

Act now to free them.

If you do not.

Consequences for you.

Are Looming.

Do not make any mistakes.

When the Grandfather Clock.

Chimes at Midnight.

The walls talk.

There is 'Evil' here.

There is Death here.

Dead people can talk, they do have a voice.

Abhorred torture has prevailed upon us.

The Dead buried within these walls.

Needs to come out and they do.

We the slain; put here,

Against our will.

The 'Blood' in our veins

Are about to 'Spill'.

We entered the 'Fray,' and we now must pay.

With our lives.

In God's name, we say, set us free.

Take us to the light.

Please do it 'Tonight'.

We will haunt you forever.

Until you do what we say.

Take a deep breath; it may be your last.

This Gripping Psychological

Thriller

Full of Twists and Turns.

'The Dead See Everything.'

Behind these walls.

The squeamish will scurry,

The brave will stay.

Take a Ride if you Dare.

Take a breath; this might give you a scare.

When you pass through the gates; 'Hell'
awaits.

This will assess your imagination over again.

There's peril within the walls.

That's Awaiting YOU!

The Dead talk

This House Can Kill

Are the steps welcoming you in?

Hope for the Best

But prepare yourself for

The Worst

Evil Lives Here

Take a Deep Breath

Table of Contents

Dedication

Lynne Walsh & Anna Giuliani

This book is for both of you.

I thank you for inspiring me.

Thanks for being there.

I am 'Honoured' to know you.

I welcome your 'Encouragement.'

The Dead see Everything.

This is No Ordinary House

These are Not Ordinary People

Decide,

Enter or Stay

Prologue

Things will happen when you least expect it. You will need all the strength and courage you can muster to enter this 'House' and if you 'Dare', there will be consequences. This is a mansion of 'successful' proportions. There are people within these walls, and they will tell you 'Horrific' stories, but are you prepared to listen? It has a journey you will need to deliberate. The House is not what it seems. Do you take a 'Gamble'? But think about what you are gambling with. It has your life. It is significant that you consider this carefully, as you do not know what will happen once you are inside the gates. Are you ready to listen to the 'Walls'? The stories will shock you. This house has stood for generations, owned by a wealthy family through criminal activity and 'Greed'. Be very assured that this house is 'Not' a tourist attraction; there is nothing wrong with the house itself, it has what has happened in it that's 'Alarming'. In an affluent neighbourhood on Melbourne's east side, a suburb called 'Hunters Hill' in the valley, an elite part of town with prominent residents such as bankers and echelons of magnates, the wealth that far stretches the 'Norm' of society could reach. Gastronomic ideals and examples of what it has been like to have everything one's heart could want in life.

The new residents, however, are not the elite; they will bring a new meaning to the leafy, tree-lined streets of

'Hunters Hill'. Comparable to bankers in another sense, these new residents could buy banks with the amount of money they have bought from crime proceeds. Not known in affluent circles, but they have reputations in other circles of society—the 'Hoods' and gangster kind of element of society—and are very well established. Their money had a very pungent smell about it and could be known as 'Blood' money. Earning money the conventional way of hard work and legitimate success is not what this couple brings to the table. They are very unconventional, and the proceeds of their earnings leave nothing to be desired. The money earned with the desire to rule and consider themselves to be a force to be reckoned with directly. With this arrogance and their feelings of how to make money, they will leave society breathless, to say the least. 'Hunters Hill' is about to take a 'Tumble' of massive proportions; await the 'fallout'.

'Terror' Awaits

The Unknown

May have a surprise for you.

Are you willing to take a gable?

Remember the last time?

You were scared.

Get ready.

You are going to be scared again.

Chapter One
❧The Wedding❧

It is a lovely day in Melbourne as we commemorate the *marriage* of Marguerite and Toby Forsyth. They were wed in the stunning Brighton cathedral, *The Lady Saint of Hope*, as the sun bathed the day in golden light. Inside, Toby, the guests, and the groom all await the arrival of the bride, Marguerite.

She arrives fashionably late, the organ striking soothing tones within the cathedral. Marguerite glides down the aisle with confidence and poise. Toby turns, glimpses her, and smiles as she walks toward him. A hush falls over the congregation. Anticipation swells.

The archbishop finally proclaims them husband and wife. Applause erupts as the couple exits *The Lady Saint of Hope*. Everything has gone smoothly, until now.

The guests gather in the car park, forming a convoy to the reception venue in Melbourne's western suburbs. They snake through the freeway, a symphony of honking horns saluting the newlyweds. Spirits are high.

But this will be no ordinary reception. These are no ordinary people.

The reception venue is far from glamorous, it's a rough pub in *Blackville*, a seedy part of town frequented by criminals. Fitting, considering most guests share ties to Melbourne's underworld. These are Toby and Marguerite's people. Associates. Criminals. Thieves. Gangsters.

Toby's best man, Augustus, nicknamed *The Henchman*, is notorious. Violent. Vicious. A man with a razor in his back pocket and no hesitation to use it. They call him *The Slasher*.

You'd expect a wedding to be civil. Joyous. But these people are far from normal.

As the reception begins, drunkenness takes hold. Tension simmers. Augustus walks to the microphone to deliver his speech. Minutes in, drunken hecklers interrupt. He warns them.

"Do not make me come over there to sort you out," Augustus growls into the mic. "Because there will be blood, and it won't be mine."

The heckling continues.

Toby leans toward Marguerite and whispers, "Look at Augustus… I know that look. He's going to explode. This won't end well."

Sure enough, chaos erupts.

Chairs and tables fly. Bartenders duck for cover. A brawl breaks out, and Marguerite and Toby join in without hesitation. Marguerite grabs a bottle of bourbon, smashes it against the bar, and lunges. With one savage swipe, she slits the throats of two hecklers.

They die instantly.

Toby, impressed, kisses her amid the carnage.

"Oh, my darling," he says proudly, "successful work! I am so proud of you."

Augustus unleashes his razor, slashing those who supported the hecklers. The room is soaked in violence. No friends among thieves.

Augustus returns to the couple.

"Sorry about that," he offers gruffly.

"No need," Toby responds. "They got what they deserved. They underestimated you."

"Oh Augustus," Marguerite chimes in with a wicked grin. "I loved cutting those bastards' throats. I'd do it again, happily."

Augustus chuckles.

"Toby, that's one hell of a woman you've got."

The bloodshed ends. Marguerite fetches the shaken bartenders.

"We're thirsty," she says calmly. "Pour the drinks, and make them doubles."

The bartenders comply, trembling. Drinks are served. Augustus takes the mic once more—no more interruptions this time.

His speech is laced with sarcasm, referencing the brawl. He ends with a toast and a surprise announcement:

"Toby and Marguerite have purchased a mansion in *Hunters Hill,* yes, where the rich and famous live. Quite the upgrade from the slums of the west. But trust me, they'll make their presence felt."

Now the bride and groom take the stage.

Toby is candid. He talks about the mansion but offers no details, only this:

"The house will undergo a drastic makeover. Marguerite, Augustus, and I, yes, *The Henchman*, have joined forces. We are a trio now, and we're going to change things. *Hunters Hill...* the name is fitting. Because we intend to do some hunting of our own."

Marguerite steps up next and stuns the room.

She declares her full allegiance to this new partnership with Augustus. She calls it a *perfect alliance*. Her eyes burn with fervor.

The storm outside brews. The night is electric. Nothing is conventional. Not the people. Not the wedding. Not their plans.

We like to think society is predictable. Safe. But think again.

We make assumptions, but we are not profilers. And you're going to need all the skills you can muster to figure these people out. Don't assume you know who they are. You don't.

Look deeper.

Some secrets are never told. But you're about to hear them.

Chapter Two

❧The Journey of Adolescents❧

To understand this couple, their violent unity, their mansion, and the *terror* about to be unleashed, we must go back. Before the wedding. Before the killings. To the seeds of their darkness.

Toby and Marguerite went to the same high school, but never met. Toby admired her from afar. Too shy. Too withdrawn. Both were introverts. Loners.

One cool Saturday afternoon, fate intervened.

Toby had just finished football training. Walking along the southern edge of the park, he heard sobbing. Behind a broken wire fence, he saw her: a girl curled on a bench, weeping into her lap.

He stepped closer.

"Hello, Miss… my name is Toby. Are you okay?"

She looked up. Recognition flickered in her eyes.

"I've seen you around school," she said. "But I never knew your name."

Toby sat beside her, placed a gentle arm on her shoulder.

"Want to tell me what's wrong?"

She hesitated.

"Two boys stopped me," she said hoarsely. "They demanded money. Said if I didn't give it, they'd rape me. I ran. I found this bench."

Toby's voice softened.

"I'm so sorry that happened. No one will hurt you while I'm here. What can I do to help?"

"I have problems at home," she sobbed. "I don't know what to do."

"Talk to me," Toby said. "That's the first step."

She did. Everything. Her voice trembled. His face paled.

And then he replied:

"I understand. Because it happened to me too."

"What?" she gasped. "To boys?"

"Yes. To me. If you promise not to tell a soul, I'll tell you what happened."

She promised.

And in that moment, a pact was born. Two broken souls. Kindred in trauma.

Toby came from wealth, but not the honest kind. His family's fortune was soaked in crime, corruption, and blood money. He became a stand over man.

Marguerite came from poverty. Raised in abuse and neglect. A life of wounds, without healing.

Together, their broken pasts did not mend. They fermented. Festered. Hardened.

What should have healed became the foundation for something else.

Control. Power. Vengeance.

They will not be controlled. They will *control you,* and manipulate you. Only to their benefit.

They are fractured. And their familiar pain will shape their future.

They did not escape the horror of their upbringing. They embraced it.

Are you ready to hear their stories?
Are you prepared?

Because what comes next will shock you.

And it's only just begun.

Chapter Three
❧The Peril of the Removalist❧

Now that the wedding festivities are over, Marguerite and Toby get down to the business of moving furniture into the mansion. Two removalist men and two trucks were commissioned. The removalists lugged heavy items into the house, commenting to each other that they could hear faint voices and conversations emanating from downstairs.

One said, *"It's nothing. It's a magnificent old house, but it has an air of gloom about it."*

The other replied, *"You often hear about old houses like these... people say they're haunted. I wonder if this one might be haunted too?"*

"Are you afraid?"

"There is reason... perhaps."

Still unloading furniture, the men passed a corridor and noticed a room with a heavy door frame fitted with large iron gates. Whispering to one another, they remarked how the doors looked eerily like those of a jail cell, with strange smells wafting out.

"I can't imagine what the owners use these rooms for," one said. *"In all our years as removalists, we've never seen*

a house quite like this. A bell tower is one thing... but these rooms look like dungeons. Wouldn't you say?"

They laughed nervously.

"The owners are odd," one muttered. *"The woman looks like a walking corpse, and the man, he's aggressive the way he talks."*

As if summoned, the woman, Marguerite, appeared behind them. Her face was deathly pale, her bloodshot pupils ringed with burst capillaries. Her expression was blank, her steely eyes seeming to pierce right through them. She radiated a chilling aura.

In a voice sharp as broken glass, she ordered, *"Go to the trucks and bring the six metal boxes."*

They obeyed. Returning with the trolley-laden boxes, they found Marguerite standing outside the iron-gated door, jingling a bunch of keys ominously in their faces.

"Put the boxes inside and place them on the floor."

Once again, they complied.

When they looked up, Toby stood before them, glaring with a deep frown.

"You made rude comments about our house. I don't like either of you."

"We didn't mean to offend," one of them replied. *"We just said old houses like this might be haunted, that's all."*

"And what about what you said about my wife? You called her a walking corpse."

"Yes... I said that. I apologize."

Toby's voice was low, measured. *"Do you know what a corpse looks like?"*

As they began to respond, Toby reached into his back pocket, pulled out a cutthroat razor, and in one fluid movement, slashed both their throats.

They dropped to the floor with a heavy thud.

Toby smirked. *"They won't be saying another word."*

Marguerite grinned. She lunged toward him, kissed him passionately, and whispered, *"Oh, my darling... you were magnificent. So quick, so decisive. A wonderful killing."*

Together, they unpacked the metal boxes onto the dungeon floor, chains, weapons, and high-end photography equipment. Marguerite staged the scene to photograph the corpses. They stripped the men, rifled through their pockets, collected cash and valuables, then dressed the corpses in shrouds, adding frilled collars around their necks like a mortician would.

The couple were high school sweethearts turned murderous psychopaths. The violence they inflicted was senseless, their cruelty theatrical.

Marguerite snapped photos of the men in their funeral attire.

Then the doorbell rang.

It echoed through the mansion, amplified by Toby's high-tech security system.

He dashed upstairs.

At the door stood Augustus, the Henchman.

"We have a problem, Toby. I need to speak to you urgently."

Toby invited him downstairs. Marguerite greeted Augustus.

"Hello, Augustus. How are you doing?"

"Not well. The drug deal went wrong. We've been set up. The drugs were delivered, but the suitcase they gave me, empty. So, I cut their throats with my razor."

"Where are the bodies?" Toby asked.

"In the back of my truck."

"Bring them in. We'll take them to the dungeon."

The bodies were carried in. Marguerite's eyes lit up at the sight.

Stripping the corpses, they discovered $20 million in cash, the real payment for the drugs. Toby handed Augustus his cut.

"They didn't have the drugs," Augustus said. *"They double-crossed us. That's why I killed them."*

Marguerite dressed the new bodies in shrouds and collars and photographed them. Her collection grew.

Later, she took the photos to her Dark Room, where she developed and framed them, ready to hang on the walls.

Returning to the dungeon, the trio discussed where to bury the latest victims. The house had been carefully renovated for just this purpose, walls built to inter bodies, each hidden behind layers of plaster and brick.

The two new victims were placed beside Marguerite's parents. Toby's parents were in there too.

Marguerite giggled. *"Now they all have company. Let them talk for eternity."*

This was Toby's childhood home, a place steeped in twisted memories. Officially, his parents had "moved to the UK." In truth, Toby and Marguerite had murdered them.

For years, the trio ran an empire of corruption and crime in Melbourne's west, hauling in millions.

The house? A graveyard masked as a mansion. Augustus's truck delivered the dead. Gangsters, thieves, and traitors all lined the walls, buried and forgotten, except for the macabre photographs Marguerite proudly displayed.

They had never been caught. Never even suspected.

Their wealth explained away as success; their eccentricity masked by high-society façades.

But now, they were ready to go further.

Marguerite called it "The Bucket List."

Each body ticked off. Each soul sealed.

Jewelry would be stolen or taken by force. Marguerite swore the walls still had space.

"The gullible belong here," she whispered. *"I need the thrill of killing in abundance. Let's rip their souls. Let's seal their fate."*

This was no occupation for the faint of heart. Killing was theatre. It was art.

Society? They didn't care. Wealth and status were their targets.

"The Henchman is on board," Marguerite said. *"We'll build an empire."*

Recruits would be trained. Torture rooms built. Surveillance upgraded.

They were ready.

Once rulers of the west, Toby and Marguerite now had a third in their syndicate.

The benchmark was set. The criminal Armageddon was rising.

The old adage, *"Two wrongs don't make a right"*, was now irrelevant.

Three wrongs made an empire.

Marguerite once joked: *"Hitler ruled once. Why can't I?"*

"He caused mass destruction," she said. *"I admire him. He was a hero to me."*

Toby listened; his head bowed. *"I wouldn't mind being remembered... even as the next Hitler,"* he murmured.

"You'd be excellent," Marguerite replied. *"But remember, we are a trio now. You are brilliant. Strategic. Ruthless. Augustus agrees. You're a force of nature."*

"Together," she said, *"we'll be unstoppable."*

This town would burn.

Toby's razor would return to the streets, leaving carnage in its wake.

He was carving his legacy, one body at a time.

Chapter Four
❧The Housewarming Party❧

**K**illers Among Us

This is no ordinary housewarming party. You may be invited, but you will not be welcome.

It's an underground operation, with dire consequences.

The guests will yield to our demands. Only fifteen have been invited by Augustus the Henchman, each selected for a reason. All is not what it seems.

As the guests arrive, they're greeted at the front door by Marguerite and Toby, then ushered into the Parlor, where the festivities begin. They spread out, some in groups, others as couples. Refreshments are served, along with a selection of canapés. Marguerite and Toby, appointed to serve, use the opportunity to mingle one-on-one.

The invitation stated this would be a late-evening affair, asking guests to arrive at 9:30 p.m. A special presentation was promised at midnight.

A couple, Jodie and Max, sit quietly, sipping cocktails beside an incredibly old Grandfather Clock, adjacent to a large wingback chair. Jodie notices a white sheet draped over the chair. She leans in closer and whispers to Max:

"That sheet looks like a shroud... the kind used to wrap a dead body."

The eerie sight unsettles her. She asks Max to take a closer look.

"Yes, you're right," he replies, frowning. "It *does* look like a shroud."

Suddenly, a voice calls out to Jodie. A silhouette appears in the chair, an old man. Jodie jumps back in fright.

"My name is Benjamin Woods," the figure says. "I was killed here years ago by the owners of this house. They're going to kill you too—tonight. Help me escape. Turn around and look at my photo on the wall. Do you see me?"

"Yes," Jodie and Max reply in unison. "We can see and hear you."

Shaking, Jodie whispers:

"I need the bathroom. I'm going to wet myself."

She rushes out. After using the toilet, she washes her hands. Looking into the mirror, she sees another figure behind her, a woman this time.

"My name is Melanie Waters," the woman says. "Look closely."

Trembling, Jodie obeys.

"I'm dead. I'm trapped behind this wall. I was killed by Toby and Marguerite. They put me here."

"Can you see my photo above the mirror?"

"Yes," Jodie answers. "You're wearing a shroud, like the man in the Parlor. He talked to me too. His name was Benjamin Woods."

"There are many dead people buried in these walls," Melanie says. "Marguerite photographs her victims after she kills them. Help us. Get us out of here."

Jodie stands frozen. Her breathing quickens. She grips the sink to keep from fainting. Cold water splashes her face. When she looks up again, the silhouette is gone.

Chapter Five
❧The Grandfather Clock Strikes Twelve❧

T his clock will begin to talk. The dead within these walls speak. They must warn the living. The dead see everything.

Max and Jodie are now buried behind the walls.

The villainous trio, Augustus, Marguerite, and Toby, gather after the brutal murders. They begin to plan the fate of the remaining guests upstairs in the Parlor.

"There are still thirteen left," Marguerite says.

Toby smirks. "Let's scare the hell out of them when the Grandfather Clock strikes midnight. I'll start the hologram projections. The silhouettes of the dead will move across the room. It's all ready."

The trio returns to the Parlor. Augustus pauses briefly to speak with his new recruits, the *Monks*.

"There's a special event coming at the stroke of midnight," he tells them. "Let's just call it a little project of mine. You'll see."

Back at the party, they're showered, dressed in evening wear, mingling once more.

Marguerite counts the guests. She frowns.

"There are only twelve people," she whispers to Toby. "One is missing, James Moreland."

Toby walks up to Katie and Sam.

"Have you seen James Moreland?"

"Yes," Sam replies. "He said he had to leave after getting a phone call from his wife. He apologized and left early."

"Oh," Toby nods. "Thank you. While you're here, may I ask something?"

Katie leans in.

"We were just talking about that. We heard strange noises coming from the walls. People screaming… saying things like 'Let us out.' They claimed they were killed here. They told us to look at the photos—that you and Marguerite put them there."

Toby laughs.

"That's a silly notion. You're letting your imaginations run wild. Just relax, enjoy the party. You're all here for a reason, and you'll be rewarded for your contributions."

He lowers his voice.

"We own this town. We're the envy of the underworld."

Meanwhile, James Moreland, fully aware of how devious this trio is, had sensed danger. The midnight timing of the announcement raised his suspicion. His quick exit may have saved his life.

Back in the Parlor, the formalities begin. Marguerite and Toby step up to the microphone.

"Please welcome our fearless leader… Augustus," Toby announces.

Augustus's speech is short, direct:

"Welcome, my disciples of crime. You've all contributed to our success, and tonight, you shall be rewarded. We've made billions in recent years. It's time you got your cut."

He gestures to the Grandfather Clock.

"It's fifteen minutes to midnight. Please separate yourselves. The Monks will approach with envelopes. Remain silent when you receive them."

The Monks enter the Parlor in single file. Faces covered in black mesh. Long black robes. Each holds a white envelope. They hand them out silently, standing behind the guests.

"At midnight, open your envelopes," Augustus says.

The Grandfather Clock begins to chime. The guests open their envelopes. Each card reads:

"You are all going to die."

Gasps echo around the room.

The Monks seize the guests, handcuffing their arms behind their backs. Suddenly, the room fills with projected silhouettes—faces and forms of the dead. The photographs on the walls swivel violently.

The guests are frozen in fear. Voices call from within the walls.

"We are the ones this trio murdered. Help us. They're going to kill you, too. You must try to escape before it's too late!"

Hands begin to push through the photographs. The guests stare in horror—paralyzed.

Then Toby shouts:

"Monks, strike now!"

From beneath their robes, the Monks pull out box cutters. With one swift motion, they slash the guests' throats. The bodies fall lifeless to the floor.

The Grandfather Clock chimes its twelfth and final tone— A perfectly choreographed moment of death.

Silence falls over the room.

Augustus shakes each Monk's hand.

Marguerite hands them each a white envelope.

"Don't worry," she says with a sinister grin. "These ones are full of cash. Well done."

Chapter Six
❧The Cemetery❧

Is there someone here you know? Are you searching for a missing person? Don't Walk this path. Evil lurks here. You will never come out.

"Tell me, Toby," Marguerite asks, "how did you get the sounds to come out of the walls?"

Toby replies calmly:

"I didn't. The voices you hear, they're real. They're the dead. All I did was turn your photographs into holograms. I projected them throughout the house using my computer. But the voices? That's them."

Marguerite gasps.

"I thought it was just you playing around... but you're telling me the dead *really are* speaking?"

"They are," Toby confirms. "We just have to live with it."

Marguerite thinks for a moment.

"Why don't we buy another house to live in? Keep this one for the killings. We have billions. We can afford it."

"No," Toby says sharply. "This house has everything we need. Security systems, a brand-new morgue, and privacy.

Moving would draw suspicion. Besides, we'll make more money right here."

"Fine," Marguerite shrugs. "Then why not build our own cemetery in the backyard? We've got plenty of land."

"That could work," Toby nods.

Augustus chimes in: "I'll get the Monks to help. They can be the gravediggers."

With that, plans are set. Augustus calls the Monks back for a strategy meeting.

The Funeral Parlor Heist

Augustus proposes a bold plan: midnight raids on local funeral parlors to steal coffins and transport them back to the house.

"What a brilliant idea," Marguerite says. "But first, let's prepare the backyard."

They agree to begin with the cemetery gates, placing them near the roadside for easy truck access. The graves will be dug farther back, away from prying eyes. To complete the illusion, they'll raid nearby stonemasons for headstones.

"What's a cemetery without headstones?" Marguerite says dreamily. "I'd love to look out the window and see our own graveyard, full of societies useless. A perfect view."

They calculate space. The backyard could fit two thousand bodies.

Half the Monks stay on-site to run excavation equipment.
The rest assist Augustus in the raids.

They prepare bolt cutters, box cutter blades, and alarm-disabling tools.

The raids begin.

On the first night, the Monks cut through the locks and disarm security systems with ease. Their research had paid off; the funeral parlor had just received a large shipment of coffins.

By dawn, Augustus returns in a truck filled with one hundred coffins.

"Well done," Toby says, beaming. "Magnificent effort."

The Monks unload the coffins into a massive shed on the property, where others have dug forty graves during the raid.

"Let's take a moment to celebrate," Marguerite announces.

She invites everyone into the Parlor for food and drinks.

Later, Augustus reports:

"The Monks performed brilliantly. Efficient. Precise. We should reward them."

"Bring them here," Marguerite says. "I'll pay them myself."

Marguerite, once a woman of poverty, now throws around cash with reckless ease. Her transformation is complete. She is consumed by power, emboldened by her love for Toby, and driven by criminal ambition.

But something stirs behind the walls. The dead are watching.

Toby believes he is the master manipulator, the *joker*. But who will have the last laugh?

Chapter Seven
❧The Stranded Passengers❧

Toby goes back to the dining table where Marguerite is seated and tells her what just happened. "This is an opportunity to rob these people of their money and valuables," he says. "Once they're inside, we'll lock all the doors from the outside so they can't escape. I'll grab key locks from the garage and secure the exits."

"Oh, my sweetheart husband, I adore your cunning ways," Marguerite replies. "Let's get started."

Marguerite welcomes the stranded coach passengers into their home. She reaches out to Augustus and explains the situation. "I want to bring the Monks back, we're going to need them," she says. "Any extra muscle you can organize would be beneficial. We're dealing with fifteen passengers plus a coach driver. It'll take some planning, but this is a goldmine."

She reflects on their previous success with the same number of victims. "We learned from that," she tells Augustus. "This group is just the beginning. Bigger, darker plans are on the horizon."

The coach passengers are greeted by Marguerite and Toby, then shown to their rooms, escorted by Augustus and his trusted Monks. As the guests head upstairs to settle in, Toby moves quickly, locking each door from the outside to ensure no one can leave.

"I don't want them wandering the grounds," Toby mutters. "Especially not near the cemetery."

With the guests unpacking, Augustus summons a private meeting in the Ballroom. The trio, Augustus, Marguerite, and Toby, joins the Monks for a strategic session. It's the first time the Ballroom has ever been used in this way, a room of grandeur now doubling as a war room.

Marguerite stands to speak. "Tonight, each of you will receive a universal key. While the guests are enjoying dinner, we'll give you the signal. You'll enter their rooms, take everything they own, and stash the items in the hidden cabinet behind the Grandfather Clock."

Toby adds, "Once the theft is done, I'll lock every external door. Then, we'll announce a house- wide lockdown. No one leaves until I say so."

Augustus stands, his tone dark and commanding. "We're on a special mission tonight. At 11:45 p.m., we'll gather at the Grandfather Clock. At the stroke of midnight, you'll enter the rooms and begin the killings. Show no mercy."

He pauses.

"We're unknown in the East, for now. But soon, we'll be recognized as the *leading gangsters*.

Kill with pride. Uphold our values. Respect your employers, Toby and Marguerite. We are *killers*. This dynasty must grow and prosper." His final words echo through the Ballroom:

"Now let's get to work. And more importantly, don't forget to have fun."

Chapter Eight

&The Great Robbery of Trains the Hijack&

At the Henchman's private depot, prime mover trucks are being loaded with guns and rifles for a convoy journey toward regional railway lines. Meanwhile, the Monks, fresh off their last assignment, have returned from funeral parlors with a new haul of coffins. The inventory now stacked in the shed is impressive.

With ample stocks replenished, Augustus convenes a meeting with the Monks. "Tomorrow morning," he says, "we hijack the trains. Be ready."

The new truck drivers, perched high in the cabs of their vehicles, prepare to transport their deadly cargo. The Monks, riding in the back, will guard the weaponry. For the first time, the Monks shed their signature black cloaks. Today, they'll wear civilian clothes and blend in as passengers.

Toby and Marguerite opt to stay behind, watching from their living room as the events unfold on television. They remain in contact with Augustus via mobile communication, ready to respond if anything goes wrong.

It's a bright, clear day, perfect visibility. Augustus had checked the weather; the green light was given.

The train has already departed the city terminal. The

convoy rolls out steadily, careful not to arrive too early at Bromham Railway Station, the boarding point for the Monks. The hijack is planned for the next stop: Scottsdale Station.

Inside the trucks, the Monks load their satchels with guns. The specially designed pouches hang across their shoulders, giving them quick access in close quarters. These same satchels had proven effective in past shootouts. Augustus communicates via CB radio.

"Train approaching Bromham in fifteen. Drivers, confirm location." "We're here," the lead truck radios back. "Just pulled up at the station."

"Perfect," Augustus replies. "Unload the Monks. Trucks, proceed to Scottsdale."

The Monks step onto the platform, moving like ordinary commuters. The trucks roll ahead to the intercept point. Augustus speaks again:

"Keep all lines open. I want full updates as this unfolds."

"Copy that, boss."

The Monks board the train without incident. The operation is now live. The convoy speeds toward its destination, Scottsdale Station, the place where a new reign of terror is about to begin.

Chapter Nine

✢Rival Gangs Declare War✢

Still in the ballroom, Marguerite stood tall and addressed the room.

"The 365 bodies were searched. Large sums of cash, bags of jewelry, cheque books, and signed documents were seized. I will personally forge the signatures on those cheque books. The train robbery was a success, an enormous one, and as always, we've ensured fair remuneration for your work."

She smiled. "Please meet us in the parlor, where I'll distribute your pay. You've all earned it."

All the bodies, including those recovered from Mike's truck, had been buried. The men assembled in the parlor, where they received their hefty payments. As the last coins were counted, a mechanical buzzing vibrated through the window.

Drones.

Dozens of them.

They hovered outside, capturing photos of the gang, Augustus, Toby, Marguerite, all of them. Guns drawn, the group rushed outside, shooting down the drones. Some were destroyed, but not all. Images had already been captured. Evidence now existed somewhere.

Furious, Augustus exploded. "This is gang-related. They're coming for us."

He turned to his men. "We must work together to eliminate them. They want to muzzle our business, but we'll fight them, not to our deaths, but to *theirs*."

He faced his twenty-four drivers, excluding Mike, and the monks. "Are you with me?"

A resounding *yes* echoed back.

"Good. I'll be recruiting twenty-five expert snipers immediately." Later, Augustus spoke to Toby and Marguerite.

"I need my men stationed here. They'll be living in this house for a while. We're under siege. These rival gangs know where we are, and they won't stop. We must eliminate them for good. I'll spread the word: if anyone wishes to challenge us, we've got graves waiting. That's not a threat, it's a promise."

He implemented a 24-hour surveillance roster. Snipers were placed on rooftops, ordered to shoot drones and kill intruders on sight, military precision, just like Augustus learned in the army. The gates and fences were electrified. Snipers received hand grenades and telescopic rifles for pinpoint accuracy.

This was war.

The house became a fortress.

Sleeping bags lined the windows. New recruits, truck drivers and snipers, sensed something was off. The blood-spattered walls and the looming Grandfather Clock gave it away. Once the clock struck midnight, everything would be revealed. They would soon confront not just rival gangs, but the demons that lived inside these walls.

Silence fell.
Then, the roar of motorcycles.
The first wave of invasion had arrived.

Snipers held position as bikers approached, trying to open the gate. Electricity surged, three were instantly killed. Their comrades drew weapons. The snipers fired with lethal accuracy. All were killed.

The monks rushed forward, dragging the bodies inside. They collected the motorcycles and parked them beside the coffin pile left from the funeral parlor heist. The bodies were delivered to the morgue, where Toby and Marguerite waited.

"Another dead load for you," one monk said with a smirk.

Toby dressed the bikers in shrouds. Marguerite photographed them with glee. Once done, the monks buried the bodies.

Marguerite smiled at Toby. "I now have a magnificent collection of jewelry, and you, my darling, have a collection of Harley-Davidsons. They'll sell well, though I'll let you keep one. That's only fair."

Augustus, however, wasn't smiling.

"This isn't the last of them. Once word spreads, more will come. Toby, your collection will grow."

He was right.

A second wave came and met the same end.

Augustus prepared his men. "More syndicates will try us. The bloodbath will continue. Be ready."

The cemetery filled. The roster rotated. A third gang arrived, one Augustus had clashed with before, hospitalizations, but never fatalities.

This time, he intended total annihilation. A convoy of cars pulled up. "Grenades!" Augustus ordered.

Explosions lit the night. Cars burned. Many gangsters were incinerated before stepping out. Others died on the electrified gates. The snipers cleaned up what remained with a thunderous hail of bullets.

Augustus surveyed the carnage.

"No more hospital trips for this lot," he said, turning to Toby and Marguerite. "They're morgue- bound now."

Another photo session. Another burial. Another win for the trio. The monks joked, "The cemetery is filling up nicely."

Marguerite beamed. Toby was dubbed "the new Hitler," though she thought "Frankenstein" might be more fitting. A monster of their own creation.

Later, Augustus ventured into the city.

The streets buzzed with fear. "The Henchman is on the warpath," they whispered. Rival gangs hesitated. The dead hadn't returned, and word spread fast. Augustus had set a precedent, cross him, and you end up in the ground.

Back home, he called a meeting.

"We've made our impact. Maybe they'll fade away. Maybe not. Either way, stay alert. We're targets now."

Marguerite, brimming with pride, made an announcement.

"I'm hosting a dinner tonight, for all of you. You've earned it. I'm bringing in top chefs, waitstaff, everything. Let's celebrate in the ballroom."

Augustus nodded. "Fine. But my men stay armed. Just in case."

"Of course," she replied. "Completely understandable."

He briefed the men: "Sixty of you are attending. Bring your weapons, but enjoy yourselves. This dinner is in your honor."

Marguerite gushed to Toby. "I'm wearing my finest gown and the stolen jewelry. Your tux is laid out on the bed. We'll look fabulous."

They chuckled like school kids.

"I'll move the Grandfather Clock into the ballroom," Toby said. "And we'll hang the biker photos on the walls as a tribute."

"Brilliant idea," Marguerite replied. "That's why I love you, always thinking evil."

The monks moved the clock. Photos were hung. The ballroom transformed into a macabre shrine.

Caterers arrived.

"I want seven large round tables, ten seats each," Marguerite instructed. "Of course, madam."

They decorated with fresh flowers, fine China, and linen. One caterer admired the clock. "It has... significance," Marguerite said, smiling darkly.

The kitchen, unused for years, buzzed with activity. "Everything alright?" she asked the chefs.

"We had trouble with the gas stove, but it's sorted. A magnificent feast is coming." "Good," she said. "Deliver what you promise, and you'll be tipped handsomely." Little did they know they were serving the country's deadliest couple.

Marguerite had once compared herself to Hitler, and her husband wasn't far behind. Together, they spun a deadly web. Their victims never escaped.

The killings were brutal. The terror was real. And the *Empire* stood tall, dripping in blood and laughter.

Chapter Ten

❧The Guns Are Loaded❧

Augustus had arranged the sleeping bags once again, spreading them around the parlor so the men could rest together. Standing before them, he gave his order:

"Gentlemen, I want you all to take a nap, it's going to be a long night. Your guns are in the satchels beside you, fully loaded. When you're seated in the ballroom, place your weapons beside your chairs for easy access. If anything seems suspicious, don't hesitate, draw and fire. Kill if you must. I'm counting on you. Rest well, so you're ready. Tonight, will be a night to remember."

When the men awoke, Augustus was already watching from the doorway. As they stirred, he entered with a smile.

"Gentlemen, I have a special treat for you."

He wheeled a large garment rack into the center of the parlor.

"Tonight, you will wear tuxedos. Your names are tagged to each suit, I trust they'll be a good fit. Take a shower and return here. Then we proceed to the Grand Ballroom. And remember, tonight you are gentlemen. Behave yourselves. Toby and Marguerite have spared no expense."

Clean and sharp in their tuxedos, the men returned. Augustus beamed with delight.

"Oh, my goodness, look at you all, absolutely dashing! For a moment, I forgot you were the hardened criminals I know so well. Monks, it's certainly a change from your black hooded cloaks... your 'killing robes.' You almost look like civilians."

With that, they formed a convoy and made their way to the towering doors of the Grand Ballroom.

At precisely nine o'clock, the Grandfather Clock chimed. The men gathered at the entrance. The waitstaff opened the doors and led them inside, where they were offered wine and canapés. The air was thick with anticipation; the arrival of Marguerite and Toby was imminent.

As drinks continued to flow, Augustus gave his command:

"Place your weapons beside your chairs, gentlemen. Do so with care, we'll be standing to greet our hosts shortly. No tripping, please."

At nine-thirty, the Grandfather Clock struck once. The ballroom doors opened wide.

Marguerite and Toby entered.

The men rose and applauded. A standing ovation roared across the room. Marguerite glided in, wearing a flowing ballgown adorned with glittering stolen diamonds, around her neck, ears, and wrists. Beside her, Toby stood proud in a black velvet tuxedo.

"They look like royalty," someone gasped. "The King

and Queen."

The couple moved gracefully from table to table, greeting guests with casual elegance. At their table, Marguerite leaned in toward Toby and whispered:

"What a magnificent job the caterers have done."

"Yes," Toby replied. "Spectacular. You promised them a generous tip if they delivered."

"And they have," she said with a smile. "I'll handle it."

The evening unfolded beautifully. The mood was light. Conversation buzzed, drivers, sharp shooters, and new recruits received much praise. Augustus glowed with pride; their empire having emerged unscathed from battle.

And yet…

Something simmered beneath the surface. The Grandfather Clock was ticking closer.

Was this peace only temporary? The clock struck midnight.

Suddenly, the ballroom changed.

Ghosts seeped from the walls, thousands of them, shrieking:

"We were murdered here by Toby and Marguerite! Kill them before they kill you!"

The men leapt for their guns. Bullets flew. Ghosts swarmed. Paintings swung violently. The shooters fired indiscriminately.

Three wait staff were killed in the crossfire. Others fled, screaming.

The chaos intensified.

From the photographs on the wall came voices:

"Marguerite and Toby killed us. We know about the train robbery. We were buried out back... in the cemetery."

Blood began dripping from the walls.

Marguerite screamed:

"STOP FIRING!"

The chefs burst from the kitchen, only to be caught in the crossfire. Three were shot dead.

The others ran, but took a wrong turn and found themselves at the cemetery fence. As they tried to climb it, the electric fence lit up.

They perished.

Silence fell.

The ghosts disappeared back into the walls.

The floor was littered with bullets and bodies. The photographs now lay smashed.

Augustus stood pale and frozen.

Marguerite and Toby slumped at their table; heads buried in their arms. Minutes passed.

Finally, they joined Augustus at his table. Toby broke the silence, trembling with rage.

"What the hell were you thinking, Augustus? Why did you order your men to shoot? They were ghosts. You've heard them before. They're dead. This is a disaster; we'll pay dearly for this."

Augustus stammered:

"How so?"

"Some escaped. They'll tell the story. Yes, most of the staff are dead. Yes, only three chefs were electrocuted, but some escaped."

Marguerite interrupted:

"We must act fast. The escapees can't be far. Get in the truck. Find them, bring them back. Your life depends on it."

Without hesitation, Augustus barked orders. The convoy rolled out in search of survivors. Left behind, Toby and Marguerite sat in silence.

Finally, Toby spoke:

"I know this is bad. I know this isn't how the night was meant to end. Augustus was terrified rival gangs would attack. When he heard voices... he panicked. I did too. I yelled; I was angry. I shouldn't have. I was scared."

He paused. A tear ran down his cheek.

"In all my life... no one has ever escaped. And now, they have. They'll talk. They'll ruin everything."

He buried his face in his hands, overwhelmed by the weight of the night.

Chapter Eleven
❧The Tabloid's Woe❧

The Valley Gazette Newspaper

'The Missing People'

Marguerite was now calm and composed. She gently picked up Toby's head from the table and placed her hand softly on his face.

"Do not blame yourself for what happened," she said. "It wasn't you who did this. I think we both know that whatever actions Augustus took, it would have only been in our best interest, right?"

"Yes, I guess so," Toby replied.

He continued, "Augustus made one mistake, but I've known him for years. What I know about him is his loyalty, it's genuine. And I know he'll find those people. He'll leave no stone unturned. He knows if they're not found, he'll be responsible for all of us getting caught. He won't let that happen. So, I have to trust him. We just have to wait until he comes back. I have every confidence in him."

Augustus returned. His face told a thousand stories, one of bewilderment, stripped of its usual charisma.

"We've been searching," he said, "but to no avail. I've

instructed the monks to keep looking." Toby apologized for his earlier aggression.

"There's no need to apologize," Augustus replied. "I understand why you were angry. I was so concerned we'd be targeted by gangs. The moment I heard the noises; I reacted and gave the order to shoot. I should've known better. I'm the one who should be apologizing to you."

"Well, it happened," Toby said. "We just have to move forward. If the monks find them, that's a bonus. If not, we'll deal with the consequences. We're devious criminals, we'll find a way out of any problem. The waitstaff will be too frightened to say anything."

The monks returned with no new information. The search had been extended. Still, no luck. The Valley Gazette Reports:

We, the reporters of The Valley Gazette, are deeply concerned by the escalating crime wave affecting our community. Turf wars between rival gangs have intensified. We are now seeing break-ins at funeral parlours and the theft of coffins, crimes of unprecedented magnitude.

Most recently, a rural train was hijacked. Neither passengers nor conductor have been found. Are we seriously to believe they vanished into thin air? Where are the facts, and more importantly, where are the police?

Thousands are missing. Where are they?

Crime has become an industry. A criminal economy teeming with thugs who have no moral compass. It is time for the government to step in. This is no longer acceptable. Our society is devolving into a cesspool of criminal enterprise, where people make money without honest work, without taxes, without conscience.

There is no honour among thieves. The missing must be found. The guilty must be held accountable. And the public deserves to feel safe. As long as these deviously deranged thugs roam among us, no one is safe.

We must act. We demand answers, fast.

Our newsroom has been flooded with calls from frightened citizens. And with good reason. We report on the missing because we care. We want to shake the tree and expose what's hiding in the branches. The media can bring attention to the issue, but it cannot solve it alone.

We urge you: if you see something, say something. Someone's life may depend on it. It could be your life. Or the life of someone you love.

We report it to you. You report it to the police.

Toby took a stroll around the backyard, still unsettled. To clear his head, he walked to the local store for groceries. Inside, he noticed a group of elderly women huddled in a corner, whispering behind a newspaper.

Curious, he inched closer.

"They say crime's going crazy," one of them whispered. "It's all right here in today's paper."

A chill crept down Toby's spine. He rushed to the newspaper stand, grabbed a copy, and shoved it into his grocery cart.

As he walked home, curiosity got the better of him. Passing a nearby park, he noticed an empty bench and sat down. He pulled out the newspaper and began reading.

As he skimmed through the article, his normally cold, bloodstained hands began to shake and flush crimson. For once, not from violence, but from fear.

If the press is reporting a spike in crime, are they talking about us? His heart pounded. Then, he saw the section about the hijacked train. *It's us. It's definitely us.*

He slammed the paper shut and stuffed it deep into his grocery bag. For a moment, he sat on the bench, breathing deeply, eyes wide, thoughts spiraling.

He stayed there, frozen, for nearly half an hour. Eventually, he regained his composure. He stood up, steady now, and began walking home, his mind whirring with questions.

Chapter Twelve

&The Police Investigation&

Toby enters the Parlor and finds Marguerite and Augustus sitting together, sipping coffee. Without a word, he brushes past them, stops, reaches into his shopping bag, and pulls out a newspaper. He slams it down in front of them.

"I think you should both have a read of this," he says sharply. "I'm going to put the groceries away, and when I get back, we're going to discuss this article."

He exits briefly, and when he returns, he notes two very different reactions. Augustus looks puzzled. Marguerite is calm, almost indifferent.

Toby sits down.

"So, what do you think about the article? It's obviously written about us." Augustus sighs, his voice low. "Yes, I've read it. It's... concerning." Before he can continue, Marguerite cuts in, dismissive and sharp.

"Oh, you men, you're such pussies. Lighten up!" She turns to Toby. "You were sitting next to me watching the news as it unfolded, Augustus and his men committing the crime. So why has this article got your head in a spin? This isn't breaking news, it's old news. The crime was committed a week ago, and now it's just showing up in print. Big deal. We don't care. So, get a grip, both of you, and stop worrying."

Meanwhile, the police addressed the public in an official statement:

"We are working in collaboration to ease the anxiety troubling the community, and with good reason. Loved ones have not returned home.

We want to assure the public that we are making consistent and serious efforts to find the missing and bring the perpetrators to justice. We appeal to anyone who may have any information, no matter how minor. Even the smallest detail could be the key to apprehending the offenders.

Helicopters were deployed during the incident known as the 'Train Hijacking.' Forensic teams have been combing the surrounding bushland in search of the train driver and passengers. We believe the train was full, due to several major events taking place that day in central Melbourne, events which country residents often attend via train, avoiding the congestion of city roads. Train travel is a comfortable and popular option.

We've made progress. Our forensic teams collected shoe and tire impressions along the roadside, which are currently under analysis. Based on early findings, we suspect a case of abduction, hundreds of passengers disappearing simultaneously.

We're also investigating a string of break-ins at funeral homes over the past few months. As bizarre as it sounds, coffins have been stolen in enormous quantities. This has raised significant red flags within the department. The scale of this operation points to well-connected criminal gangs executing these brazen acts with terrifying precision."

The police spokesperson continued:

"Yes, we're aware gang-related crime has escalated, a fact recently reported by the *Valley Gazette*. Media remains an essential tool for solving crimes. We urge anyone with information, no matter how insignificant it may seem, to come forward. This could help us bring justice to the victims' families.

Gang warfare is no secret. These groups are jockeying for power, trying to become the 'Top Dog.' We know they exist. We even know who some of them are.

Today, we launch Operation Snoop. This multi-faceted operation will place investigators directly in contact with criminal networks. We have specialists trained in information extraction. Moving 365 people from a train would require enormous transport vehicles, trucks on an industrial scale. Once tire impressions are fully analyzed, we'll share more.

Those responsible will be held accountable. Justice will be served. We take this seriously. Our motto remains: *To Serve and Protect*. In us, you have our devotion."

Suddenly, new information came to light.

"Our forensic lab has confirmed that the tire impressions match those of newly released *Prime Mover* trucks, recently sold by International Trucks. We've identified a buyer, a known figure in the underworld. He goes by the name The Henchman.

We urge the public not to approach him. He is considered dangerous. Detectives assigned to Operation Snoop have reported breakthroughs. Informants from the underworld have come forward, identifying two names: Marguerite and Toby Forsyth, long-known gangsters, with disturbing histories dating back to youth.

Catering staff and waiters have also shared terrifying experiences while working at the *Mansion on the Hill*, believed to be the Forsyth's recent residence. Detectives are reviewing all collected information, and we've applied for a search warrant for the premises."

The warrant has been granted.

"We can confirm that abhorrent acts may have occurred at the Mansion. I commend our detectives for their persistence in pursuing justice, especially for the local communities around *The Valley*.

Drone surveillance, captured by rival gang members, revealed a brutal assault leading to multiple gang deaths. Footage shows individuals dressed like monks burying what appear to be bodies in shallow grave sites.

Our worst fear is becoming a reality: a mass grave. Not only may the missing be buried there, but also the train driver and passengers. We must bring closure to grieving families and stop these macabre criminals."

The final orders were issued:

"The search warrant has been handed to the police sergeant. He has called a briefing for all officers, local units, neighboring forces, and riot squads, to assemble at headquarters at 5:00 a.m. sharp.

Stay alert. Be sharp. We move on The Mansion on the Hill at dawn."

The Day of Reckoning

For Marguerite, Toby, and the Henchman

6:00 A.M.

The riot squads and tactical units descend upon the mansion on the hill. A battering ram shatters the front door. Police swarm in, search warrants in hand.

They comb through every room. As the sweep continues, they hear voices… faint, ethereal...coming from inside the walls.

The dead are speaking.

Up on the fourth floor, in the last bedroom on the left, Marguerite and Toby sleep soundly, unaware of the storm brewing below.

In the Grand Ballroom, the officers stop in their tracks and *gasp*. Even the most hardened among them feel their blood chill. Bullet holes pockmark the ornate walls. Blood pools on the gleaming floor. Dirty dishes and abandoned glassware clutter long banquet tables.

"This must've been... a party," one whispers. "But what kind?" They count the chairs. There are too many.

A tilted Grandfather Clock ticks in the corner. The pendulum swings steadily. The time on its face is accurate. Blood drips down its mahogany casing.

Then, the voices again.

"Please... look at the photos that have fallen... off the walls."

They do.

Portraits of the dead. Pale faces, wide eyes, desperate stares.

"We are trapped within these walls. Laid to rest, we are not. Toby... Marguerite... and the Henchman, they did this. Tortured us. Buried us. Behind these walls, we screamed."

The pendulum swings. Violently.

"It always did... when death came. As if the clock *watched*." "Look outside the window," the voices plead.

And they do.

A cemetery. In the backyard.

"Was that always here?" an officer asks.

They step outside. The earth is freshly disturbed. Headstones still clean, inscriptions unweather. The radio crackles.

"Sergeant? We may have found the stolen headstones." "I'll meet you at the front," the Sergeant replies.

Moments later, the Sergeant stands among his officers at the edge of the backyard cemetery.

"These... these are the missing stones," he says, holding up photos from the stonemason's report. "Exceptional work. This, this is huge."

There are *thousands* of graves.

Train passengers, maybe. A plausible assumption.

Back inside, the enormity of the crime begins to crystallize. Greed. Power. Death. Disappearance. Loss. The backyard is cracked and weather-worn, evidence of heavy traffic and frequent digging. The officers, numb from the grotesque revelations, return to the station with a plan: task forces must be assembled. This horror goes deep.

They begin to leave, until the voices stop them cold. From the graves.

Whispers.

Then, coffins jolt upward, breaking through the soil.

Constable Melody *screams* and collapses. The Sergeant revives her with smelling salts. "This has gone beyond anything we've seen," he mutters. "We need forensic teams. Now."

Back inside, the search resumes.

In the Parlor, photographs line the walls, hundreds of them. All with closed eyes. All in *shrouds*. "What *is* this place?" whispers an officer.

In the corner: a pile of robes, hooded, ceremonial. "Bag them for prints and DNA," the Sergeant instructs.

In the attic, the air is colder. Musty boxes. Duplicate photographs of the dead. A string light casts a warm glow, an eerie contrast to the oppressive odor of decay.

"This place reeks of death…" Melody says, "…and something else, fear." "It's thick," Constable Hurley agrees. "This whole place is screaming." They descend again, this time into the basement.

Steel gates line the corridor. Blood splatters. Shackles on metal benches. "These are dungeons," Hurley says. "People were held here. Tortured." At the corridor's end: massive steel doors. Hurley touches them. "Cold," he mutters, pushing them open.

A morgue.

Dead silence, then, *gasps*.

Bodies. Rows of them. All dressed in shrouds. The Sergeant pulls out his phone. No reception. "We need to go outside."

They retrace their steps, back to the main house. Finally, he makes the call. Reinforcements are dispatched.

On the way out, they find a shed. Hurley breaks the lock. Inside, coffins. Dozens. Stolen from funeral homes.

"Get serial numbers. Contact every funeral home and stonemason. We're going to tie all this together."

At the Police Station Interview rooms. Occupied.

Marguerite.

Toby.

Augustus.

Each is placed in solitary. Observed through one-way mirrors. Their demeanors: shaken, agitated.

Marguerite, withdrawn.

Toby, smug.

Augustus, cold and arrogant.

The detectives confront Augustus first.

Evidence:

Fifteen stolen trucks.

Drone footage of the burials.

CCTV of funeral home thefts.

His shoes, identical to the ones worn during the train hijacking.

He resists. They overpower him. The shoes are bagged for evidence.

"You're done, Augustus," a detective says. "We've got you. DNA, footprints, witnesses. You're going back to prison."

Augustus is livid. Curses fly.

The tests come back. A perfect match.

"And there's more," the detective says. "Informants. Drones. Witnesses. You're being charged with the abduction and murder of the train passengers and driver."

Augustus is taken to holding. He flips the bird on the way out. Marguerite and Toby get the same treatment.

The Chef survived.

The wait staff testified.

They saw the electrocutions. They saw the shrouds.

They saw it *all*.

"You're under arrest," the detectives say.

Both are taken to separate cells. The Sergeant and Superintendent walk the halls.

First, Augustus.

"Welcome home," the Sergeant says. "Miss your old mates? Hope they miss you too."

Then, Toby.

"Smug now," the Sergeant snarls, "but let's see how you hold up in general population."

Finally, Marguerite.

Hunched in the corner.

"Time to think about your sins," the Superintendent says. "No husband to protect you now. Let's see how the other women feel about what you did."

Chapter Thirteen

❧The Bodies Are Falling Out of the Walls❧

A special task force and forensic team are dispatched to the mansion.

When they arrive, the local police are already on scene, grim-faced and shaken.

"We don't envy the task ahead of you," a constable mutters. "It's gruesome. You have our sympathies… and good luck."

The team begins with the cemetery.

The coffins are scattered, twisted as if violently ejected from the earth. They're strangely intact, fresh, almost new. The lids are screwed shut. No bodies visible.

The headstones? Also new. And eerily blank, no names, no dates. From the mansion, voices pierce the still air.

Set us free. We are behind the walls.

A member of the forensic team whispers, "Is this place haunted?"

Inside the house, the teams get to work. Crowbars in hand, they rip open walls. The first body falls out.

Screams echo through the halls.

Some are skeletons. Others, fresh. Faces locked in terror.

Thousands of photos hang on the walls. One forensic tech, pale and stunned, mutters: "These are the victims... the people in the walls."

Mandy, the head of forensics, takes a photo of a recently discovered body. She searches the walls.

Over an hour passes.

She finds it.

"It's an exact match," she gasps. "The frilled collar. The shroud. Someone photographed them after death... This person was murdered and memorialized like a trophy."

The house is a labyrinth of horror. The team documents everything. Room by room. Wall by wall.

The Grandfather Clock sways violently, pendulum slashing the air. The chimes ring erratically, loud, frantic.

"Is the clock... warning us?" one officer says.

The blood-covered walls whisper of torment. The bodies, Mandy says, were killed before they were entombed. And judging by the scale,

"There could be thousands more."

Police swarm in. The scale of the crime is staggering. The missing from the community. The train hijacking. All possibly tied to this hellish house.

"Augustus the Henchman. Toby. Marguerite," a

detective says grimly. "They're in custody now."

Police scour the grounds. In the cemetery's shadowed slope, rookie officer Madelene Westerman lets out a scream.

She's found a ditch filled with knives, bloodied, rusted, some pristine. Nearby, saw blades glint in the dying light.

Her stomach churns.

"I never imagined this on my first case..." Constable Brendan Hurley comforts her.

"You're doing what you set out to do, help people. The evidence you're collecting will put monsters away."

He leads her back into the house. Downstairs, they enter the morgue.

A massive saw blade dominates a blood-stained table.

"That's it," Westerman gasps. "That's the blade from the ditch." She nearly collapses.

"It was used to dismember people, wasn't it?" Hurley nods.

"You're right. And now, thanks to you, we have more proof. You've done good, Westerman." In the Grand Ballroom, the Grandfather Clock shakes more violently than ever.

"It's like it's trying to *speak,*" Westerman says. The dead are speaking now.

"They killed us. The trio, Augustus, Toby, Marguerite. Tell our families. We are here... within these walls."

Tears stream down Westerman's cheeks. "Do you hear them?" she asks Hurley.

He nods solemnly. "Yes." The voices continue:

"At midnight, with every chime, someone died. Except Betty and George... they were killed during the day. We saw everything. A chef tried to escape; he was electrocuted by Toby. Others got away. But we've been trapped... until now."

Westerman steels herself.

"Hello. My name is Constable Westerman. I want you to know, the trio who did this have been arrested. They will never hurt anyone again. I promise."

A hush settles. Sighs echo from the walls.

Thank you.

Suddenly

The Grandfather Clock Stops.

The room holds its breath.

No more swaying. No violent tremors. No whispering ticks.

The pendulum hangs still... lifeless.

80

Dead, just like the people in the walls.

Constable Westerman turns to Hurley, eyes wide with eerie certainty.

"The clock... it had a spirit. I think it witnessed everything. It was trying to *shake it out.* Trying to scream. That's why it moved so violently. Now... the spirit is gone."

Hurley doesn't speak right away. He just stares at her.

He paces, then halts, lost in thought. Is it his imagination... or does Westerman possess something he's never seen before?

Something *otherworldly.*

She had silenced the walls. Calmed the dead. Interpreted their cries.

Hurley exhales slowly.

"You've been nothing short of incredible," he finally says. "Whatever it is... psychic, spiritual, or just gut instinct, you've done first-class police work. And you've brought peace to the damned."

They continue their grim sweep of the house. Room by room.

On the top floor, they enter a bedroom, frozen with unnatural cold. Wedding photos line the walls. Toby and Marguerite, smiling.

But the air is heavy. The air *knows.*

A voice cries from inside the wall:

"LOOK UNDER THE BED!"

Westerman doesn't hesitate.

Hurley steps forward, eager to take the lead.

"I've got this, Westerman," he says, a spark of determination in his voice. Maybe he's been feeling like a sidekick too long.

He gets down flat on the floor. Dust clings to his uniform as he reaches under the bed. His fingers touch something.

A book.

He pulls it out, sits on the edge of the mattress beside Westerman, and flips it open. "It's a diary," he mutters.

The voice returns, urgent:

"READ IT. YOU MUST READ IT."

Hurley gulps. The leather cover is old, cracked. The name "Marguerite" is etched inside. He begins reading aloud.

His eyes widen.

He stops, gasping.

"This is it," he says. "This is everything."

Westerman leans in. "What is it? What does it say?"

"It's a full confession. In her own words."

He reads aloud from the pages, disturbing entries documenting murders, methods, names. The Henchman. The Monks. The truck drivers. And always, *Toby*.

"To my darling husband," one passage reads, "your ideas of restraint and execution are simply divine. Every night, I read these back to you. You smile like a child on Christmas morning."

Hurley snaps the book shut.

"This woman read *murder* like bedtime poetry."

At that moment, a long, drawn-out sigh echoes from within the wall. A release.

Westerman gasps. "That was her spirit. It's relieved. Someone finally *knows*." She raises her voice.

"You're free now. Go toward the light." The cold vanishes.

So does the presence. Hurley stares at her in awe.

"You can really talk to the dead..."

He pulls out his phone and calls the station.

"Sarge? It's Hurley. Forgive the interruption, it's your day off, I know. But this can't wait. We've had a breakthrough."

The Sergeant's voice comes through. "Go ahead,

Constable."

Hurley speaks quickly. Urgently.

"We found Marguerite's diary. Voices told us where to look. Under the bed. It's a full confession, detailed. Every murder. Every player. The Henchman, the monks, the drivers. She even names Toby as the mastermind of their torture routines. She loved taking photos of the dead. They dreamed of building their own morgue. Their own cemetery. She even wrote about starting a criminal empire that would 'never be rivaled.' It's all there. In her own hand."

Silence.

Then:

"Stay put. I'm coming to the house."

Within twenty minutes, the Sergeant arrives. He steps into the hallway and calls out:

"Constables! I'm here!" Westerman and Hurley meet him. Hurley presents the diary.

The Sergeant flips through it slowly, expression darkening.

"This isn't just evidence. This is the key. This will put them away, forever." He turns to Westerman.

"Outstanding work, Constable. You've earned a commendation for this. Exceptional." To Hurley:

"And you as well. You've been with us for years, but this… these changes everything. You *broke the case.*"

He gathers the team in the ballroom.

"We've endured the unthinkable. A Grandfather Clock violently shaking as if possessed. Coffins ejecting from the earth. Voices from walls. I'm not a man who scares easy… but I'll admit, this house… it shook me."

He stares at the walls.

"It's time to call in someone… holy."

Father O'Reilly arrives the next morning. He's escorted to the Sergeant's office.

Coffee is offered. Politeness exchanged. Then the truth comes out.

The Sergeant doesn't hold back. He tells the Father *everything,* the bodies in the walls, the voices, the confessions, the diary.

"I've seen horrors, Father. But this... this was evil wearing a mask of ritual and civility. They *enjoyed* it."

Father O'Reilly's expression doesn't waver.

"Then it's time," he says. "This house must be cleansed. The souls of the dead… must be set free."

Chapter Fourteen

❧The Exorcism❧

The following morning, the Sergeant and Father O'Reilly meet at the front gates of the *Mansion on the Hill*. They pause before entering. Strange flickering lights pulse behind every window, eerie, almost unnatural. They exchange a look, gather their courage, and approach the front door.

Father O'Reilly reaches into his cloak, retrieving his Bible.

As they step onto the porch, unsettling noises echo from within. Low murmurs. Unseen footsteps. Father O'Reilly begins reciting passages from Scripture. Suddenly, a turbulent gust of wind swirls around them with violent force. He sprinkles Holy Water across the porch.

The front doors swing open with a thunderous crash.

Inside, shadows move unnaturally, silhouettes floating midair. The Sergeant narrows his eyes.

SERGEANT *(to Father O'Reilly)*

This is... most peculiar. The forensic team cleared the house. All the bodies were removed to the coroner's office. How do you explain this?

FATHER O'REILLY

It is my presence that stirs them. You'll see far more before this is over.

The voices inside grow louder, panicked, angry. Father O'Reilly begins a more fervent incantation, flinging Holy Water into the air.

DISSONANT VOICES (unseen)

You must leave! Intruders! This is our house. You do not belong here. Leave, or we will take your lives.

SERGEANT

What is the meaning of this?

FATHER O'REILLY

The spirits are trapped here, Sergeant. They haven't crossed over. Something... is keeping them bound.

He raises the Bible high. Suddenly, WHAM, an unseen force hurls him backward.

SERGEANT

(rushing to him)

Father! Are you alright?

FATHER O'REILLY

Yes... yes, but this is more than restless spirits. There's a Demonic presence here. It controls them, dominates them.

He reaches beneath his robes, pulling forth a wooden cross from around his neck and raises it toward the grand staircase. He chants forcefully. A black, misty silhouette materializes.

FATHER O'REILLY

The Lord is here with you, your Savior

BLACK SILHOUETTE

I will kill you if you persist. Leave now.

At that moment, a side door bursts open, and a wave of icy air floods the room. A figure, dark and angular, moves into view. It's a *Grandfather Clock*.

SERGEANT

That clock... I've seen it here before.

Now it's back. The clock hands spin wildly before stopping, 9:20 a.m.

FATHER O'REILLY

(checking his wristwatch)

That's the exact time.

The pendulum swings. The chimes begin. Violently. The clock shakes.

SERGEANT

One of my constables, Madelene Westerman, said the clock stopped when the bodies were removed. She said... *the clock had died.*

FATHER O'REILLY

The demon has moved into the clock. It's using it as a vessel.

VOICES (from the walls)

We were murdered... buried in these walls. We can't escape. Help us!

The demon rises. The walls quake. Plaster cracks and crumbles to the floor.

SERGEANT

What is happening?!

FATHER O'REILLY

The demon's furious. It will destroy everything to protect its domain. The other spirits cannot escape until it is defeated.

The *Grandfather Clock* jumps violently across the floor. Lights flicker madly. The demonic force lashes out, striking

Father O'Reilly again, this time with a piece of ceiling plaster crashing into his temple. He falls, bleeding.

VOICES (screaming)

Get us Westerman! Get us Westerman! Only she can free us!

The Sergeant makes a quick decision; he drags Father O'Reilly out to the porch. He slams the door shut, pulls out his handkerchief, and wraps it around the Father's wound.

FATHER O'REILLY

I'm sorry... I failed.

SERGEANT

No, Father. You tried. Now we need help.

He pulls out his mobile, dials.

SERGEANT

Constable Westerman, thank God you answered. We need you. The demon... it's controlling the spirits. They're calling out for you.

WESTERMAN (on phone)

I'm on my way. Take care of Father O'Reilly. I'll fix this.

Westerman arrives swiftly, kneeling beside them.

WESTERMAN

Tell me everything.

SERGEANT

You wouldn't believe it. The Grandfather Clock, it's possessed. The demon's keeping the other spirits trapped. They need *you* to set them free.

WESTERMAN

Understood. But first, I'm calling an ambulance. That's a nasty head wound. Ambulance sirens wail. Father O'Reilly is whisked away.

SERGEANT

The house is silent now. Too silent.

WESTERMAN

That's because the demon no longer feels threatened. But I'll change that.

Inside the house, they return together. The demonic presence stirs. Shadows flicker. The Grandfather Clock begins to tremble again.

WESTERMAN (to the Clock)

You've returned. You were still yesterday... I thought the victims had found peace. But you're restless now, because the demon is back. It controls you. It suppresses the others. That ends now.

She steps forward; voice steady.

WESTERMAN

Demonic spirit, I demand you leave. Your presence is unwanted.

Be far. Be far from here.

These poor souls need not thee.

Go to the Light, Demon, or else hell waits for you.

The room fills with warmth. The black silhouette shrieks and dissipates. The Grandfather Clock stops. The pendulum stills. The spirits... are gone.

WESTERMAN

They've crossed over. It's done.

SERGEANT

You were brilliant, Constable. You handled this perfectly. Since joining the force, your record has been exemplary.

WESTERMAN

Thank you, Sergeant. That means the world. But I must add, Constable Hurley has supported me from day one. I owe much to him.

SERGEANT

Well said. And now?

WESTERMAN

Now, I'd like to visit Father O'Reilly at the hospital. See

how he's doing.

Chapter Fifteen
✿The Coroner's Inquest✿

Family and friends gathered to hear the findings of the coroner's report. Due to the sheer number of people involved, a suitable venue had to be secured; one that could accommodate thousands. The Gladstone Arena was chosen.

Most of the police officers and forensics teams had volunteered their time to attend. From early morning, thousands began pouring into the arena, anxious to secure a seat, hearts heavy with the need for closure.

At the center of the arena, with notes in hand and a solemn expression, Coroner Michael Stanford stepped up to the microphone. A hush fell over the crowd as he began to speak, trepidation thick in the air.

Michael Stanford:

"Good afternoon, and may I extend a warm welcome to you all.

Please allow me to begin by offering my deepest condolences to the families, friends, and loved one's present. This has been an immensely complicated process for everyone involved, an ordeal of unimaginable scale.

Over the past six months, we have undertaken meticulous forensic analysis. The task required consulting experts from across the country. This work has been conducted with the utmost respect and dignity for every individual.

There are no easy answers. No quick fixes.

But I can confirm this with certainty: none of the deaths were accidental. Every life lost was taken deliberately. Every case, murder.

It would be impossible, in a gathering of this size, to go through each individual finding. I understand you may have wished to hear the outcome concerning your loved one. I truly do. But due to the enormity of this tragedy, a more private approach has been arranged.

Each individual case has been thoroughly recorded, and a file has been created for every victim. These reports have been placed in sealed envelopes, organized by surname.

You may collect them at your convenience. A reception desk has been set up in the west wing of this facility, where names are listed alphabetically.

Let me be clear, this was not the result of a natural disaster. This was not a tsunami, nor a wildfire.

What we are dealing with is mass murder, an atrocity committed in our very city on an unprecedented scale.

The perpetrators responsible for these heinous acts have been apprehended and are currently in police custody. For some, that may bring a measure of solace. For others, I understand, it may do little to ease the pain.

In closing, on behalf of myself and all the teams involved, we are truly and deeply sorry for your losses.

I hereby declare this inquest formally closed."

As he stepped away from the microphone, silence lingered. Then, slowly, movement returned to the room; grief, quiet and personal, walking hand in hand with those seeking answers.

Chapter Sixteen

❧The Trial – Judgement Day❧

Judge Edward Vernon Blake has been commissioned to preside over the proceedings of this historic murder trial. Due to the unprecedented scale and gravity of the crimes, the case will be conducted in the Federal Supreme High Court of Australasia. A panel of King's Counsel appointees will also preside, with strict adherence to impartiality, uninfluenced by the intense media coverage that has engulfed the nation. The trial will be decided solely on evidence and facts under federal law. All decisions will be final. No appeals. No retrials.

Security is at its peak today as the largest trial in the country's history begins. Twenty-nine shackled perpetrators are being loaded into heavily armored transport vehicles at the local police station. Outside, furious residents hurl obscenities, bottles, and cans at the convoy. The streets of Melbourne's communities are still raw with grief and rage, mourning the unspeakable horrors inflicted by these criminals.

Today is Judgement Day.

Thousands line the streets around the Supreme Court, unified in sorrow and outrage. The courtroom is expected to reach full capacity. Media swarms the perimeter; reporters, photographers, television crews, all converging to cover this momentous event. Helicopters buzz overhead like frenzied sharks.

Judge Edward Vernon Blake arrives, escorted by armed guards. Media personnel attempt to rush his vehicle but are held back by a heavy police presence. The atmosphere is electric, tense, volatile. The people are hungry for justice.

As the transport convoy arrives, the crowd erupts again, jeers, curses, a sea of hatred. The vehicles descend a steep, secured driveway under the courthouse. A massive iron gate slams shut behind them. Armed guards with rifles and machine guns stand alert. The authorities expect retaliation, possibly even riots. So far, order holds.

Inside, metal detectors and screening stations ensure only the innocent enter. The courtroom swells with nervous anticipation. Families of victims, neighbors, the curious, and the nosy pack the benches. Idle chatter buzzes, whispers of guilt and theories, opinions shared without restraint. But today is not about opinion.

It is about facts.

The King's Counsel enters. A hush falls. Then, Judge Edward Vernon Blake makes his solemn entrance.

All rise.

The defendants, now forty-two in total, are ushered to the dock. Silence tightens like a noose. Eyes fix on the accused. Tension thickens.

Judge Blake addresses the court.

"There will be no jury today. This trial has been tainted by media frenzy. Therefore, the King's Counsel and I will serve as judge, jury... and executioner."

He glares at the defendants.

"Make no mistake, I am not here to be intimidated." The Accused

Marguerite Forsyth looks disheveled, defeated, sunken eyes, pallid skin. The holding cells have clearly taken their toll.

Toby stands with puffed-up arrogance, peacock-proud, steel-eyed. He seems to believe he's untouchable.

Augustus, the Henchman, looks drained, his once-commanding presence now a flickering shadow.

The Monks sit hunched, reclusive, expressions vacant. They are afraid. Their day of reckoning has come.

Judge Blake addresses them as a whole:

"You are heinous dictators, carbon copies of Hitler himself." Gasps ripple. Journalists scribble feverishly.

"To the families in attendance," the Judge continues, "what you are about to witness is graphic, disturbing. I know you've seen nothing beyond sealed envelopes from the inquest. Today, you will see the truth, ghastly and evil."

The Diary

The first piece of evidence is Marguerite's diary. Judge Blake holds it aloft. "Marguerite Forsyth, do you recognize this?"

"Yes," she replies. "That is mine."

"Then by your own admission, you are the author of this diary, an explicit, meticulous account of the murders. Cutthroat razors. Electric saws. Shootings. A morgue on your premises. A cemetery in your backyard. Even the train robbery."

"This is not fiction. This is confession."

Marguerite explodes in rage.

"I was forced to write it! Toby made me! He threatened to kill me. Augustus, he made me take the photos. They're evil, not me!"

Toby jumps to his feet, shouting. The Judge slams his gavel.

"Enough! Both of you are doing an excellent job of burying yourselves, just like your victims." He turns back to Marguerite.

"You're a compulsive liar. That is the absolute truth." The Monks

The Judge addresses the fifteen Monks. "Stand."

They rise, overwhelmed. Peter Wilson steps forward.

"Yes, Your Honor. We were the workhorses. But Marguerite, she planned everything. Augustus hired us, but she gave the orders."

"We and the Truck Drivers, were ordered to shoot the train passengers." The crowd erupts.

"Murderers!"

The gavel crashes down. "SILENCE or you'll be removed!"

AUGUSTUS

The Judge now focuses on Augustus. "Stand, Augustus."

Augustus rises, sheepish.

"Do you know what perjury means?"

"Yes, Your Honor."

"Good. Because you just claimed you know nothing about truck hire."

He plays a surveillance video showing Augustus walking into the International Truck Company. Pauses it.

"That's you, aren't it?"

"I didn't hire any trucks," Augustus stammers.

"No; you *bought* twenty-five. Here's the signed receipt." Augustus stammers again. Silence.

"You used them to transport bodies from the train to the

Mansion on the Hill. Drone photos and police statements confirm it."

"Let me remind you: surveillance doesn't lie. Photographs don't lie. You, Augustus, you do." The courtroom chuckles and murmurs. The tide is turning.

The Photographs

The Superintendent takes the witness box.

"Your Honor, the Mansion walls were covered with photographs of the dead. All dressed identically, in burial shrouds with frilled collars. It was... macabre."

The Judge turns back to Marguerite.

"What a twisted little creature you are. Your obsession with photographing the dead, dressing them up like grotesque dolls, is vile. You're not powerful. You're sick. A depraved liar with a foul imagination."

Toby's Turn Looms

Toby squirms, attention-starved. But Judge Blake knows his type, smug, cocky, weak under pressure. He lets Toby simmer.

"Let him stew," the Judge thinks. "His turn is coming."

It's nearing midday. The Judge announces recess. Court will reconvene at 3:30 PM. Chaos in the Courtroom

As officers attempt to remove the accused from the dock,

chaos erupts. The Monks and Truck Drivers lash out, fists flying, screaming accusations at one another. Toby and Augustus join the brawl.

The Riot Squad storms in, batons, pepper spray, tear gas. An all-out war explodes in the courtroom. The squad overwhelms them, dragging the brawling gang members into the holding cells.

Order is restored.

The Judge is notified: the prisoners are secured.

Outside the Court

Nearby cafés fill with courtroom visitors.

At Pellegrino's Pasta House, a conversation begins.

"Have you heard about Betty and George Parks?" a woman says. "They were my neighbors. One day Betty said they wouldn't be at the community tea; they were going to visit new neighbors down the road. I've been watching their driveway. Their car never came back. It's been gone for months."

Conversations of this very nature ripple through cafes and restaurants across town. Friends and loved ones discuss those who never returned home. The court case has rekindled widespread anxiety.

DINER #1 (whispers):

What we heard today… it's terrifying.

DINER #2:

We may never see them again. It's foul play, no doubt.

COUNTRY HOUSE – DINING ROOM – SAME TIME

Dorothy Sponeck, cousin to missing Betty Parks, breaks into tears at the table. Her best friend, Daisy Graham, comforts her.

DAISY (softly):

Please don't cry, darling. The truth will come out. It's painful, I know. But Judge Edward-Vernon Blake; he'll get to the bottom of it. He's kind… but ruthless in his pursuit of the truth.

DOROTHY (sniffles):

He called them "compulsive liars." That's something, isn't it?

DAISY:

Yes. It is. We just need to be strong. Come, we must return by 3:30 p.m.

SUPREME COURT – AFTERNOON

The courtroom swells again. The crowd, now nourished and hydrated, settles in. Judge Blake and the King's Counsel take their positions.

JUDGE BLAKE (sternly):

What you are about to witness will be disturbing. If it's

too much, I urge you to leave now.

Nobody moves.

JUDGE BLAKE (continues):

The identities of two undercover operatives can now be revealed:

Sergeant Thomas-Ethan Brown and Superintendent Alan Baxter.

They have served with distinction, as has Coroner Michael Stanford. Their efforts have brought us here.

Joining us now, Constable Madelene Westerman and Constable Brenden Hurley. Constable Hurley, you may proceed.

CONSTABLE HURLEY:

Good afternoon.

The events we uncovered at the Mansion on the Hill… were horrific. We found a homemade cemetery in the backyard.

Coffins jutted from the earth. I heard voices, spirits of the dead, trapped within the walls. They named their murderers: Marguerite Forsyth. Toby Forsyth. Augustus, known as "The Henchman."

These voices led us to unthinkable discoveries.

He pauses, visibly disturbed.

CONSTABLE HURLEY (cont'd):

Inside the house, dungeons, morgues, macabre photos on the walls.

Coffins packed into a shed. And when the forensic team pulled down the walls… Bodies spilled onto the floor.

The courtroom gasps. Some vomit. Chaos ensues. Hurley steps back.

CONSTABLE HURLEY (regretful):

Despite the Judge's warning… I must end my testimony here.

CONSTABLE MADELINE WESTERMAN:

I understand your reactions. I vomited too.

Sergeant Brown was with me at the time. I had to sit and collect myself before continuing.

The room calms.

CONSTABLE WESTERMAN (cont'd):

We dredged the swamp near the mansion, following a tip from the Coach Company.

A coach had broken down nearby. The driver radioed for help. Toby Forsyth offered them shelter.

A sharp gasp from the dock. Toby buries his face in his hands.

JUDGE BLAKE:

Oh? Cracking now, Mr. Peacock-plumed, arrogant Toby Forsyth?

He leans forward.

JUDGE BLAKE:

You've stood before me before, in Melbourne, on charges of rape of a minor. You told people your parents moved to the UK. Lies.

You buried them… in the walls of their own home.

Toby glares back, death in his eyes.

JUDGE BLAKE (cont'd):

Yes, Mr. Forsyth. DNA matched. Your mother. Your father. You're not so smug now, are you?

Marguerite whispers to Toby.

MARGUERITE (confused):

What's he talking about?

JUDGE BLAKE (snaps):

Silence! I wasn't addressing you, Marguerite, but listen closely. This involves you too.

KING'S COUNSEL:

We have new evidence.

During the train robbery, a young couple were picnicking nearby.

They recorded their outing… and the gunfire. The movement around the halted train. Footage. Real-time footage.

The criminals in the dock stiffen, glancing at each other.

KING'S COUNSEL (raising remote):

We'll now play the video. Be warned.

The video begins. Gunfire. Trucks. Movement. Screams.

Augustus slumps. His face appears on the screen. The crowd erupts.

CROWD (shouting):

That's him! He killed my family! Bastard!

JUDGE BLAKE:

Enough! Step outside if needed. Otherwise, silence!

No one moves.

MARGUERITE (snarling):

You idiot, Augustus! You didn't even see the couple filming?

The Judge slams his gavel.

JUDGE BLAKE:

Stop the video. Now!

The crowd whispers. She's done him in. She's incriminated them both.

From the back, soft sobbing, the couple who recorded the footage. Fear now grips them.

JUDGE BLAKE (gently):

Court liaison, please attend to them.

HOLDING CELLS – SHORTLY AFTER

Marguerite and Augustus are separated. Officers record everything.

MARGUERITE (furious):

You ruined everything! I told you to be alert. Now we're done for.

AUGUSTUS:

If I'd seen them, I'd have shot them.

MARGUERITE:

But you didn't. That video… we're finished.

Every word is captured. Delivered to the Judge.

COURTROOM – LATER

The Judge returns. Calm. Controlled.

JUDGE BLAKE:

I have new evidence. A recording. Listen.

The courtroom holds its breath. Augustus' voice plays, confirming his intent to kill the couple.

JUDGE BLAKE (gravely):

The couple, thankfully, left the courtroom before hearing this.

Toby, shattered, listens in silence. Marguerite, his wife, betrayed him. The criminal empire unravels.

COURTHOUSE – THUNDER ROLLS

A crack of thunder. Lightning flickers. Shadows dance on courtroom walls. The gangsters in the dock sit in gloom, pondering a bleak future.

JUDGE BLAKE:

The King's Council and I will now deliberate. Bailiff, escort the accused to their cells.

The trio is led away, defeated and broken.

JUDGE BLAKE (firmly):

Court will resume at 9 a.m. sharp tomorrow.

Chapter Seventeen

&The Verdict&

*T*hursday morning. 8:45 AM.

The day the community has been waiting for.

They arrive early. Quiet, orderly. The courtroom is packed to capacity once again, every seat filled, every breath held. It's going to be a tense wait.

Outside, the sun glows warmly. The gardens of Court A are in full bloom, roses blush with color, and ivy cascades in slow, elegant spirals across the forecourt entrance. A strange calm settles over the crowd. For a moment, nature's beauty softens the grim anticipation.

But make no mistake, this day carries weight.

The verdict to be delivered will ripple through history. A moment of closure. A reckoning. The loss endured by this community is permanent, the scars etched deep. Time may eventually dull the pain, but the heartbreak? That will linger forever.

REST – IN – PEACE.

The King's Counsel enters, robes sweeping the floor, their attire more ceremonial than the day before, an homage to the Crown and the seriousness of this final act.

Then, silence falls.

Judge Edward, Vernon Blake enters the courtroom. He bows to his colleagues, respectful, resolute. He wears a scarlet robe and the traditional bench wig, exuding gravitas. Authority radiates from him. Justice personified.

The audience, entranced. This isn't an ordinary trial day. This is Judgment Day.

Every person in attendance feels it. The words echo silently in their minds. The atmosphere grows heavier with each passing second.

Eyes shift to the dock.

The accused enter, Augustus at the front, followed by his motley band of miscreants. Gang leaders, traffickers, tormentors. Their empire? In ruins. The war is over.

The scars of battle are visible, but the real damage is spiritual. The community watches them, unified, unbreakable. No weapons are needed. The power of good people, united in grief and resolve, is overwhelming.

The accused feel it. They're shrinking under the weight of it.

Their eyes, sunken. Their expressions, defeated. The criminal bravado that once defined them has vanished.

They haven't been broken by rival gangs or betrayal from within. They've been broken by justice.

By the truth.

By the people.

Today is the day someone finally pays.

Lord, hear our prayers.

Judge Blake rises.

"I commend and applaud all the families, friends, and loved ones who have attended this trial, not just yesterday but today. That takes courage. That takes commitment.

I know your loss is immense. I know your grief is overwhelming. I swore an oath to uphold the law and serve the people.

Today, I honor that oath.

The evidence presented, repulsive, disturbing. Unspeakable atrocities. Barbaric torture. Lives taken not by chance, but by deliberate, cruel acts.

These victims, lured, manipulated, and discarded. They were innocent. And now, someone must pay.

My colleagues and I have meticulously examined every detail: testimony, forensic reports, countless hours of investigation.

Our judgment has not been swayed by media, nor by the court of public opinion. Only by facts.

Only by truth.

I will now deliver the verdict."

He pauses. The courtroom stills.

Television cameras zoom in. Photographers raise their lenses. Recording devices click on. The Judge turns to the dock.

"The accused will rise."

They do, slowly. As if gravity itself resists them. They are shadows of their former selves. Defeated. Hollow.

"You are hereby sentenced for the crime of First-Degree Murder. Life Imprisonment.

No parole.

No appeal.

The crimes you committed, despicable. Heinous. Unforgivable. You are no longer *the accused*.

You are *the convicted*." The courtroom erupts. Applause. Cheers. Tears.

A frenzy of flashbulbs as reporters broadcast the moment live. Justice, at long last. Families embrace. Strangers hug. The crowd pours out into the street, shouting: "Justice has been served!"

Outside, it's a carnival of emotion. Joy. Relief. Celebration.

Back inside, the convicted are led to the holding cells, defeated, shackled, silent. Soon, they will be transported to prisons across the country. Judge Blake's final instruction: separate them.

Forever.

The verdict is fresh, mere minutes old. But its impact will last a lifetime.

Chapter Eighteen

❧The Incarceration❧

A small prison van pulls into the courthouse forecourt. Marguerite Forsyth stands at the entrance, flanked tightly by security guards. Shackled. Tawdry. Vexed. Dressed in standard-issue prison attire, worlds away from the designer ballgown she wore just months ago in her Grand Ballroom. A devastating fall from grace.

It's believed Marguerite has been separated from her husband, Toby Forsyth, since the verdict was read. No contact allowed in the holding cells overnight, by direct order of the Judge. The last time she saw Toby; they were seated beside each other in the dock. Now: nothing. The isolation, cold and calculated, gnaws at her. Rage. Humiliation. Helplessness.

Her destination: Barwon Women's Correctional Facility. Notorious. A prison for the worst of the worst. Fitting.

Marguerite is bundled into the prison van. The court guards complete the transfer paperwork. Inside the vehicle, she is handcuffed to a metal bar. A female guard leans in and whispers with icy glee:

"We heard you don't mind female company. Word is, your sex life's been quite the talk of the trial. Let's just say, you'll be very popular in there. Prepare for the ride, sweetheart."

Another guard blows her a kiss before slamming the van doors shut.

Marguerite is alone. Anxious. Petrified. The drive is long. Her head slumps forward, crucified in chains, arms stretched like Jesus on the cross. The guards' words echo, venomous in her ears.

She remembers her past.

The courtroom stripped her bare, her secrets paraded before the nation. The abuse she suffered as a child, her mother and father raping her, again and again. And now… it's happening all over again. History repeats. A living nightmare, resurrected.

She remembers telling Toby everything on a park benches that cold morning, when she was young, crying, broken. Now she's back in that space. Worse.

The van hits rough cobblestones. Marguerite is thrown from side to side. The handcuffs bite into her wrists. She wishes for death.

She deserves this, she thinks. The corpses she ordered dumped into trucks. The lives lost at her command.

Then, silence.

The van pulls to a halt. The doors open. Sunlight blinds her. Four towering women in dark grey suits, like lumberjacks or bodybuilders, wait at the gates. They unshackle her, then drag her by the hair into a stone-walled office.

A prison officer stares her down.

"We know everything about you, Bitch. Stand on the white line and answer my questions. Intake procedure. Play nice, and it won't get worse. But don't expect mercy. We watched the trial. We read the papers."

Marguerite obeys. A voice behind her asks:

"Why are you here, Bitch?" She hesitates.

CRACK. A baseball bat smacks her arm.

The officer circles her. Wielding the bat like a sword.

"I'm Officer Quinn. That question came from Officer Wheatley. You took too long. You don't get to pause."

Another woman, Officer Braddon, slaps her across the face. "I'm Officer Braddon. You'll learn quick."

A fourth officer steps close, whispering in her ear:

"I'm Officer Briggs. I like doing naughty things to women. I hear you do too." Marguerite's voice trembles.

"I... I'm here because I murdered people." Briggs smirks.

"No gold stars here, honey. Strip. Let's see what you've got."

Shaking, Marguerite removes her blouse. Her skirt. Left in only her underwear. Briggs barks:

"All of it, Bitch." She freezes.

CRACK. The bat slams her leg.

Briggs kneels. Slowly pulls down Marguerite's panties. Quinn unclasps her bra. Mocking gasps.

"Gorgeous tits," Quinn sneers. "The inmates are going to love you." Marguerite flinches.

"Yes, madam."

SLAP. A wooden spoon crashes against her face. "I'm *Officer* Quinn. Got it?"

"Yes, Officer Quinn. I'm sorry." "Learn fast, Bitch."

They strip-search her, inside and out. She's been touched by women before, her own mother, but this is something else. A grotesque ritual. A warning.

They drag her past the cells. Inmate's whistle and howl. "Fresh meat!"

"Who's the new Bitch?"

Officer Briggs unlocks six cells. Six inmates step out. Privileged. Snitches. Bribed for favors. They follow toward the showers.

Marguerite is shoved inside. Naked. Trembling. The Officers lean against the wall, watching.

Enter Helga Schultz, muscular, brutal, commanding.

"You've arrived. I'm the Top Dog. You do what I say. Understand?"

"Yes... I will obey."

Helga throws a bar of soap at her feet. "Pick it up."

Marguerite hesitates. But obeys. She bends.

And then the assault begins.

Helga strikes first, knocking her down. The six inmates' swarm. A pack rape unfolds. Brutal. Relentless. The Officers laugh and chant.

"Give it to her good!" An hour passes.

Marguerite lies on the tiles. Broken. Barely conscious. The inmates smirk.

"You got screwed good, Bitch."

The Officers escort them out, except Helga. She kneels beside Marguerite, stroking her hair.

"You were a good screw, love. That was your welcome to C Block. Pay me for protection, and things might change. But right now, you're at the bottom. And that's where you'll stay. For now."

Helga exits.

Marguerite slumps in the corner. Forlorn. Frightened. Powerless. Her empire, burnt to ash. Her criminal syndicate, shattered. Everyone turned on her.

Then, a voice down the corridor. "Forsyth!"

A shadow looms.

An enormous woman stands at the bars. Arms folded. Authority radiating from her. "I'm Vera. The inmates call me Vinegar Titts. Get up, Bitch. Say hello." Marguerite obeys.

"I know who you are," Vera continues. "You didn't think you'd get caught, but here you are. Some of these girls lost family, people *you* killed. You're not safe. But I *can* protect you… for a price. Give me your canteen privileges. But I can't guard you in my sleep."

She leaves.

Marguerite, more shaken than ever, takes it all in. Everyone knows everything. Her only weapon now? Money. And manipulation.

I need to pick the right target. I know how to deceive. I'm a planner. Survival comes first. Power will follow.

She lies on her bunk. Scheming. Always scheming.

The lunch bell rings. Cells open in regimented order. Roll call. Inmates line the halls. Military precision, by order of the Governess.

Reputation is everything.

In the dining hall, Vera appears behind Marguerite. The servers are inmates. Bribes are obvious. Food swaps hands with nods and glances.

Marguerite's plate is pathetic. She frowns.

"Don't question it," Vera whispers. "I'll explain later." They sit. Marguerite remains silent, listening.

A group of inmates discusses a new program in the recreation room, art, needlecraft, photography.

Marguerite lights up.

"Photography? That would be wonderful." The table goes silent.

A voice snaps:

"What? You gonna put us in shrouds and take our photos, Bitch?"

Marguerite gasps. Bows her head. She realizes, her obsession with photographing the dead has been made public.

Vera intervenes:

"Change the subject. Now." The mood lifts, barely.

Marguerite finishes her meal. "May I leave?" she asks.

"Not yet," Vera replies. "You leave when I say. Learn to speak only when spoken to. You're not in charge here. Not yet. Keep your mouth shut."

Marguerite complies. The fall is complete.

The dainty, feminine qualities that once seduced powerful men now attract predators. She's a target. A toy. A pawn.

But she's survived worse. And she's not done yet.

Chapter Nineteen

❧The Monks on a Mission❧

MANSION ON THE HILL

Prison vans roll up the grand, blood-stained driveway of the Mansion on the Hill. Several officers bark orders as inmates are separated with eerie precision.

NARRATOR

As per the direct instruction of Judge Edward-Vernon-Blake, the prisoners would be split, sent to two different facilities, unbeknownst to each other.

The Monks and Toby Forsyth are loaded into one van, destined for Pentridge Prison.

The Truck Drivers and Augustus the Henchman are directed into another, bound for Farnsworth Melbourne Detention for Men.

MANSION GATES – MOMENTS LATER

The iron gates creak open. The two vans diverge like fate itself is choosing sides. Neither group knows of the separation.

PENTRIDGE PRISON – ARRIVAL BAY – LATER

The van screeches to a halt. Doors burst open.

Toby steps out, shackled and confused.

TOBY (naively)

Where are the other guys? I thought they were behind us... No answer. Only silence.

The Monks disembark beside him, hoods gone, faces exposed. They're marched into the induction area.

A gruff Prison Officer leans in.

PRISON OFFICER

Well, well. Look who we have here. Toby Forsyth. You've been busy, huh? Made the news reels, even hit the tabloids. Celebrity criminal now, mass murderer, they say.

(off his silence)

Here's the good news, Toby. All your criminal mates are in here too. I'm sure they'll give you a proper welcome. The Warden's already dying to see you.

Toby shudders, sensing what's coming.

STRIP SEARCH ROOM – CONTINUOUS

The Monks are stripped, fingerprinted, and mocked by smirking officers.

PRISON OFFICER #2

No black robes. No hoodies. No masks. (smiling cruelly)

Just you now. The real you.

PRISON OFFICER #3

Most of you were small-time. Petty theft, vandalism... But now? Full-scale murder.

Big leap. Big-league welcome. One Monk gulps.

MONK #1

What do you mean by... welcome?

PRISON OFFICER #2

Ah, glad you asked.

The men here, they've got... needs. Sexual desires.

The Monk's face flushes a deep red.

MONK #1

You don't mean... with other men?

PRISON OFFICER #2

Bingo.

And advice, son: don't drop the soap in Block B.

The Monk breaks into sobs. Laughter echoes around him.

WARDEN'S OFFICE – SHORTLY AFTER

Toby is escorted in.

WARDEN BROWN

Ah, Toby Forsyth.

We haven't met before, but welcome to *my* prison. The Warden stands tall, a sadistic glint in his eyes.

WARDEN BROWN (CONT'D)

Judge Edward-Vernon-Blake asked me personally to look after you. Said you're never getting out.

Ever.

He gestures to the barred window.

WARDEN BROWN (CONT'D)

Tell me, what do you see?

TOBY (quietly)

A... graveyard.

WARDEN BROWN

That's right. Familiar?

TOBY

...It does look familiar.

WARDEN BROWN

Of course it does.

It looks like *your* backyard.

Where you buried innocent people beneath stolen headstones.

(smirking)

So, I got you a little something. Boys?

The door swings open. A trolley rolls in, covered by a black cloth.

WARDEN BROWN

Strip.

Toby hesitates, then complies. He sits in the chair, facing the door.

WARDEN BROWN

Now. Let's reveal your gift.

The cloth is pulled off, revealing a granite headstone, freshly carved with:

TOBY FORSYTH – 1981–**

Here Lies the King of Death**

WARDEN BROWN

Surprise.

It's from the same stonemasons you stole from. Donated in your honor.

(beat)

We're keeping it in storage, until you're ready to use it.

The Warden smiles wickedly. He turns to his guards.

WARDEN BROWN

Leave us. Actually... No. Stay.

Strip.

CELL BLOCK B – LATER

Toby, bloodied and broken, is led through the corridor. Inmates whistle, catcall, blow kisses. One shouts:

INMATE

See you in the showers, Toby!

They laugh. Toby curls inward. His eyes are hollow. He sees shadows of his past staring back at him.

NARRATOR

So smug he once was... with his mansion, his victims, his backyard cemetery. But now, he has seen his own grave.

Justice.

Revenge.

Served.

PRISON CELL – MOMENTS LATER

Toby lies in a fetal position, shaking.

NARRATOR

He placed headstones above the innocent. Now his name rests above his own head.

CELL BLOCK – LUNCH BELL RINGS

The prisoners line up. Toby joins them, trembling.

He hopes to sit with the Monks but they are nowhere to be seen. A voice calls out from a table:

INMATE #1

Forsyth! Over here.

Toby recognizes some faces, vague, distant memories.

TOBY

How you doing, fellas?

INMATE #2

We're good.

But you won't be.

The bravado rises in Toby's chest again, false confidence.

TOBY

Oh yeah? Is that so?

INMATE #3

You lagged on us, years ago. You remember that?

INMATE #4

We do.

Their eyes burn with vengeance.

NARRATOR

Lunch came with an unexpected side dish, *revenge*.

Dessert?

A big slice of humble pie.

LUNCHROOM – LATER

The Monks arrive late, take what scraps remain. They sit opposite Toby, surrounded by predators.

They glance at Toby. He feels the stirrings of a conspiracy.

NARRATOR

Rebellion was on the menu.

TOBY'S CELL – NIGHT

Toby weeps. He remembers Marguerite. Their mansion. The dreams of children that never came.

NARRATOR

They once spoke of laughter, children running upstairs. But instead, they chose murder. And now, darkness.

A shadow moves at his door. The lock clicks.

WARDEN BROWN (O.S.)

Today is a special day.

The door creaks open. The cold air of fate enters. Toby backs into a corner, trembling.

NARRATOR

He once ruled like a king. Now, his kingdom is a cell. And his throne, a cement floor.

The Warden steps inside. The door slams shut behind him. Silence falls across the prison.

NARRATOR

Judgment Day isn't coming. It's already here.

The snitches thrive. The killers plot. Karma is a banquet and Toby's the main course.

No henchmen. No wife. No more hiding.

Only what he gave to others now coming back in full.

Chapter Twenty
•The Workshop•

(Interior: Prison Cell, Day. The inmates, wide-eyed and eager, listen closely. The voice of authority cuts through the stale air.)

WARDEN (O.S.)

Toby! You're a bit of a maintenance man, a handyperson of sorts, isn't that correct?

TOBY (Mutters)

Well… why do you ask, Warden?

WARDEN (O.S.)

I've got a little job that needs attending to, and I think you might be the right man. We've just built a workshop adjacent to the West Wing. I believe you'd be perfect to run it.

TOBY *(Speechless. Thinks. Then cautiously.)*

Why would you give me such an honor? I've only just arrived… surely, someone else is more worthy?

WARDEN (O.S.)

Oh, don't you worry about that. *(Laughs.)* You've been nominated by many inmates. They're looking forward to assisting you. I'll personally oversee your progress.

(Beat.)

And remember what my *fantasies* entail, don't you, Toby?

TOBY *(Stunned)*

You mean… sexual favors?

WARDEN (O.S.)

Yes. Got it in one.

(The officers flanking the Warden snicker knowingly. They're in on it. They always are.)

TOBY *(Turns pale. Anguished.)*

What if I refuse?

WARDEN (O.S.)

You *can't*, Toby. It's non-negotiable. You don't get a say. I look forward to visiting you… in the workshop. And when I demand my favors, you will *oblige*. Or suffer the consequences.

(Beat.)

In fact, I feel like a favour *right now.*

Scene Shift: Corridor – Dragging Toby

Officers yank Toby by the collar. His feet scrape the floor. Inmates hoot and heckle from their cells.

INMATE 1

Ohhh, going to the Warden's office, Goldie Locks?

INMATE 2

Watch out for the paperclips, mate! You'll be bending over soon!

(Laughter erupts. Toby's tears fall freely.)

Scene: Warden's Office – Horror Unfolds

Toby is thrown to the floor. Paperclips lie scattered before his eyes like landmines.

TOBY *(Panicked)*

Please… I don't want to do this. I'm married. I—I don't do things with men…

(The Warden's smile is a slow, predatory curl.)

WARDEN

And yet… here we are.

(The filing cabinet opens with a metallic groan. Out comes a pair of large pinking shears. Officers descend. Clothes are torn. Toby is stripped, beaten, raped, first by the officers, then by the Warden himself. Blood. Bruises. Despair. He is dragged to the office window.)

WARDEN

What do you see, Toby?

TOBY

(The faintest whisper) The graveyard… again…

WARDEN

That's right. Just a gentle reminder. Disobey me, and you'll *rest* there, permanently.

(Toby nods, defeated. The Warden smiles.)

WARDEN

Drag him back. Slowly. Let the men have a look.

Scene: Cell Block B – Parade of Shame

Toby is paraded like an animal. A collar around his neck. Naked. Broken.

INMATE 3

Well, well... someone's had their cherry popped!

INMATE 4

Cute bottom, Goldie. The Warden must've loved it. *(Whistles, howls. Toby doesn't react. He's beyond reaction.) At his cell, the officers hurl him onto his bed.*

OFFICER 1

Thanks for the afternoon, Toby.

OFFICER 2

We'll be seeing you again. Better come up with something for the Workshop.

(They leave. The door slams shut.)

Scene: Inside Toby's Cell – Broken Silence

Toby curls up. There is no medication. No relief. Only agony. Cold, unrelenting agony. His pillow is damp with tears. His mind replays the horror on a loop. He mutters to himself:

TOBY

I must obey... I must stay alive.

The Warden knows… everything. The graveyard. He'll never let me forget.

He sits up. He must plan the Workshop.

Scene: Corridor – Enter Larry Lovelace

A trolley squeaks along. The flamboyant figure of Larry Lovelace stops at Toby's cell. He peeks in.

LARRY LOVELACE

Books? Magazines? Reading material? What's your fancy?

Toby turns; his face battered.

TOBY

Who… are you?

LARRY

Larry Lovelace, portable librarian. Also known for other… pleasures. I wear lace panties. The men love it. Even the Warden's had me.

He gives a playful wink.

LARRY (CONT'D)

Care to make a booking?

TOBY

(Stunned, polite)

Uh… pleased to meet you. I'll think about it. But… do you have paper? I need to write something.

LARRY

Of course! A journal and felt-tip, coming right up.

He hands over the supplies.

LARRY (WINKS AGAIN)

Let me know when you're ready for… pleasure.

He wheels off. Toby stares after him, horrified, then breaks down.

Scene: Later – Toby Plans

Toby writes, feverishly. Ideas for the Workshop. A poster campaign to win over the inmates. He knows Larry will be useful. He must play it smart. Befriend him. Use him. He requests more paper, poster-sized. Larry delivers, with a leer.

Toby drafts late into the night. Lightning flashes. Thunder cracks.

Morning Routine – Prison Showers

Bell rings. Orders barked. Inmates march. Toby is cautious. Vulnerable. Naked among predators.

But, miraculously, no attack. Just sounds of others in action. He survives this round.

Scene: Back in Cell – Still on Guard

Toby dries off, trembling. He thinks:

TOBY (V.O.)

Today, I dodged it. But tomorrow? I'm still number one. Still the target.

He stares at his posters. His project. His only chance to stay alive. To matter. To be left alone.

TOBY (V.O.)

If the Warden likes what I've done… maybe… just maybe… I'll get a reprieve.

INT. PRISON CELL – MORNING

LARRY LOVELACE appears with his trolley. TOBY greets him politely.

TOBY

Hi Larry.

LARRY *(beaming)*

Oh, indeed I will, Toby. It will be a pleasure, anything for you, Toby. I'm here to please you.

TOBY, refraining from reacting to Larry's advances, reaches under his bed and pulls out a stack of posters.

TOBY

I have the posters ready. Would you be so kind as to distribute them to the prisoners for me, please?

LARRY

I will deliver them right away, Toby. You can certainly rely on me.

TOBY

Thank you, Larry. I do appreciate your enthusiasm. Have a wonderful day! Speak with you again soon.

LARRY exits. TOBY exhales in relief and lies back on his bed, staring at the ceiling.

TOBY (V.O.)

I'm so glad I wasn't targeted in the shower this morning. Some of the other guys were, but they enjoy that. They've become immune to the sexual behavior. It's relentless. Every single day.

Shadows begin to form again in TOBY'S cell, a daily, monotonous haunting. The largest of them is unmistakably THE WARDEN. TOBY's heart races.

THE WARDEN (O.S.) *(in a friendly tone)*

Relax, Toby. It's okay. I just want to know if you've finished the project, I asked you to do.

TOBY *(with strength in his tone)*

I have indeed, Warden.

TOBY reaches under his bed again, this time pulling out a neatly wrapped file inscribed with "The Warden." He passes it through the cell bars. The officers do not enter his cell.

THE WARDEN

Great work, Toby. I'll review it this morning and get back to you by lunchtime.

The WARDEN and his officers leave suddenly. TOBY is stunned.

TOBY (V.O.)

I thought for sure they were going to drag me back to his office. Another round of abuse. Another beating.

Maybe today will be a good day... but how long can it last?

DINING HALL – SHORTLY AFTER

The breakfast bell rings. TOBY joins the lineup as doors unlock. The hall is half full, and the line is shorter than usual. He's offered a seat near a wall with a view to the prison yard.

TOBY (V.O.)

Strange. Being offered a seat? I better not ruffle any feathers.

He accepts the seat, politely.

TOBY

Thank you.

LARRY LOVELACE brings him coffee. Inmates around the table glance at TOBY.

INMATE

Do you know Larry?

TOBY

Not personally. He wandered past my cell with reading supplies one day and introduced himself.

Giggles and smirks go around. No remarks. Suddenly, a noise from outside the window draws TOBY's attention.

He stands. Outside, he sees THE MONKS, with shovels, digging graves.

TOBY (V.O.)

What are they doing?

Graves… just like at the mansion. But here? Who authorized this?

A heavy dread clouds his face.

TOBY (V.O.)

The Warden. It has to be him.

A fellow inmate nudges TOBY.

INMATE

Get in line, man. Breakfast time.

TOBY obeys, getting back in line.

INMATE 2

Aren't you the guy running that new workshop?

TOBY

Yes. The Warden asked me to manage it.

INMATE 2

We've been talking. We think it's a clever idea. We all want in.

TOBY can barely believe it. Yesterday they wanted him dead. Today, they're talking to him.

TOBY (V.O.)

Maybe I'm out of danger, at least for now.

DINING HALL – LATER

The men sit. Conversations start.

INMATES *(in turn)*

Murder. Murder. Same here.

They turn to TOBY.

TOBY *(casually, flippantly)*

Same.

Cheerful banter follows. Then the dining hall door opens. THE MONKS enter, ignoring TOBY, placing their shovels against the wall.

TOBY (V.O.)

They used to work for me. Now they won't even look at me.

The man beside him stands.

JOSH

Leave it to me.

He approaches the MONKS, speaks briefly, then returns.

JOSH

Name's Josh, by the way.

TOBY

I saw you talking to the monks. What happened?

JOSH

I changed their minds. Expect one of them to come over before the end of breakfast.

TOBY

Thank you. Is there something you'd like to do in the workshop?

JOSH

I was a carpenter. Good at making cupboards, wooden boxes—all that.

TOBY

You're in charge of carpentry, Josh. You earned it.

A MONK approaches.

MONK

Toby... we've been angry. But it's time to bury the hatchet. We'll talk to the others. Maybe things can go back to the way they were.

Judge Edward Vernon-Blake sentencing us all to life, that hurt. No wonder we blamed you.

TOBY holds his tongue, though bitterness flares inside.

TOBY (V.O.)

The monks used to answer to me. Now... everything's changed. The Trio is shattered. No one knows where the others are, and no one cares.

Friendship here? That's a fantasy. Enemies are everywhere. A Venus fly trap, just waiting to devour you.

TOBY

I saw you from the window. Digging. Just like the mansion...

MONK

The Warden summoned us. He told us not to talk. Said if we did, the graves we dig would be our own. I'm not risking it, Toby. My lips are sealed.

TOBY

Yes, I've been to his office. I know the truth. He made me look at a headstone, with *my* name on it.

MONK

He knows everything, Toby. Even asked about the caskets at the mansion. He's going to haunt us with that knowledge.

TOBY (V.O.)

Oh my god. The shed... the caskets... He's been there.

This is bad.

DINING HALL – MOMENTS LATER

The breakfast bell rings. Silence falls. THE WARDEN enters, flanked by over a dozen officers. The air turns to ice.

THE WARDEN

All prisoners, gather at my feet. Sit on the floor before me.

A scramble. A circle forms. Surprisingly, THE WARDEN smiles. THE WARDEN

Thank you for gathering. I have good news. A new project is beginning here, and you'll all benefit.

There'll be something for everyone.

I'd like to formally introduce the manager of our new workshop, Mr. Toby Forsyth. Step forward, Toby.

TOBY, nervous, steps beside him. THE WARDEN extends a hand. They shake.

THE WARDEN

Congratulations, Toby. Excellent work. Your program is approved. I'll work closely with you to get the supplies and products needed.

When the workshop is complete, we'll celebrate. Yes… I'm even considering *alcohol.*

A ripple of stunned smiles spreads across the room.

TOBY (V.O.)

He said alcohol.

THE WARDEN

Gentlemen, I bid you a good day.

He leaves. The inmates remain seated, stunned.

INMATES (to Toby) Hey mate, excellent job! Three cheers for Toby!

A cheer erupts. The men return to their cells. LARRY LOVELACE passes by, smirking.

LARRY

Toby, I can offer you pleasure for what you've done for us all.

TOBY *(grinning)*

I'll take a rain check, Larry.

TOBY (V.O.)

Not even Larry can spoil this mood.

A truce with the monks. Respect from the inmates. This has been a *wonderful* day.

I thought everyone would turn against me. But they didn't. They trust me now. It's a start.

A small step, but a real one. Something I can build on.

Chapter Twenty-One
❧The Wardens Meeting❧

*T*oby returns to his cell with a smile tugging at his face. He can hear the buzz of inmate voices echoing from other cells, a strange hum of curiosity and cautious optimism. Lying on his bed, he reflects on yesterday's breakfast.

TOBY (V.O.)

It was a win, in a way.

Inmates from my block are starting to engage with me. They're interested in the activities I arranged for the Workshop program.

Maybe calmer waters are ahead. God knows I need them.

My depression's deepening, anxiety climbing, and I was close—*too close*—to ending it all.

But the Warden... he seemed pleased with what I've put together. Maybe this will help. Maybe morale will rise.

Maybe... I'll start to feel human again.

But behind the scenes, something is being hatched. A ploy. A twist. One Toby won't see coming.

The Warden has a plan. A *comprehensive* plan. But it's not for the good of the inmates. It's for himself.

Toby's appointment as Manager of the Workshop shifted everything overnight. Yesterday, he was the hunted.

Abandoned by the Monks after Judge Edward-Vernon-Blake locked them away. No one would even speak to him.

Now?

Suddenly, he's flavor of the month. A local celebrity. Even the coldest inmates nod in his direction.

But will it stick?

The twist, orchestrated by the Warden himself, is designed to test Toby's vulnerability.

Toby may feel useful now... but the debt of the Trio's crimes still hangs thick in the air.

Powerful people, both high and low, lost loved ones. That debt will be repaid. In full.

Toby just hasn't realized it yet.

7:30 AM.

The wake-up bell has already sounded.

Toby is dressed, bed made, when shadows fall across his cell door.

Three officers appear, thumping their truncheons against the bars, startling him.

OFFICER #1

The Warden requests your presence. Private meeting.

Toby's heart skips. Sweat beads on his brow. His legs tremble.

TOBY

But... we just saw him yesterday. At breakfast. He spoke to all of us in the dining hall

OFFICER #2 (smirking)

Yeah. Funny how fast things change around here. Nothing is what it seems, sunshine.

OFFICER #3

Grab your notebook from under the bed. Yes, we know where you keep it.

Never forget, you're being watched. No privacy rights. Not yet.

OFFICER #1

Come on. Don't want to keep the Warden waiting, do we?

Toby grabs the notebook. His cell door slides open. He follows the officers down the corridor.

Other inmates press their faces to the bars, hungry for gossip.

INMATE (shouting)

Oi! The Warden must be *horny* this morning! You've been chosen, *Bum Boy*!

Have a lovely time, tell us all about it!

TOBY (muttering)

Yeah... no privacy here. Not even a damn secret thought.

The three officers knock on the Warden's door.

WARDEN (inside)

Only enter if you're good looking.

They laugh and enter. Toby follows.

WARDEN

Ah, my favorite boys. And yes, you're all looking *very* good today. Now, leave us. This is a private meeting.

The officers leave without question. Toby is alone now. Unease creeps in.

TOBY (V.O.)

He's going to ask for sexual favors again. I can feel it.

I'm powerless to stop it.

Just another pretty face to him.

WARDEN

Take a seat, Toby. Relax.

And to clarify, I *won't* be asking you for sexual favors this morning. That's already been handled.

TOBY

Handled...? I—I don't understand.

WARDEN

You missed it. The signs.

The three officers who brought you here?

They took care of my needs. We had a delightful time. Now I'm a bit exhausted... so let's get down to business.

WARDEN

I've decided to expand the Workshop.

Not just B Block anymore, I want inmates from *all* blocks involved. What do you think?

TOBY (hesitantly)

That's... an incredible idea, Warden. I designed the program to be inclusive, but I didn't think

WARDEN

You'll have what you need, Toby. Money's not an issue. You just focus on success.

There's a glimmer of sincerity. A strange turn in the Warden's demeanour.

WARDEN

We'll be meeting inmates from other blocks in the yard today. And afterward, I want to show you the new Workshop.

It's the largest purpose-built Workshop in any prison across the United States. Funded by American interests. They're watching us closely.

TOBY

You're... serious?

WARDEN

Very. I need you to lead this.

You're smart. Dangerous, yes, but intelligent. This is your redemption arc.

TOBY (nervously)

Thank you, Warden. I—I'll make it a success.

WARDEN

Good. But remember, security first.

Everyone in that yard, including *you,* will be shackled. Different blocks, different crimes.

Block A: child killers. Block F: mass murderers. Block G: terrorists.

He doesn't mention Toby's classification.

WARDEN

Coffee?

TOBY (eyes wide)

S-Sir...? You're offering *me* a cup of coffee?

WARDEN

You're one of the boys now. But don't tell a soul.

A knock. The three officers return, pushing a trolley of coffee, cake, biscuits. Toby is speechless.

WARDEN (smirking)

Morning tea with handsome men... how sexy can it be?

Toby sits quietly. Sheepish. Sips his tea. Takes a slice of cake. Uses a napkin.

WARDEN

Once we're done, officers, shackle the inmates from *every* block. Bring them to the yard. Carefully.

These men are monsters. One wrong move and it's mutiny.

OFFICERS (in unison) Understood, Sir.

There's a buzz inside the prison. And outside.

Word on the streets: the gangland vacuum is forming. The Trio is behind bars.

The wolves are circling.

A call comes through. The inmates are assembled in the yard.

WARDEN

Bring Toby.

Toby hears it. Loud and clear. He takes a breath.

WARDEN

We've got your back, Toby. You're not alone.

Toby is rattled. The officers return, carrying chains.

OFFICER #1 (whispers)

We'll be gentle.

You might even like it. Haven't explored bondage with you *yet*, Toby.

WARDEN (laughs)

Tempting idea.

Let's save it for later. Focus, boys.

Toby is bound. Blindfolded. Escorted to the elevator. He's touched—fondled.

VOICE

You don't know who it is, do you? Makes it more exciting.

TOBY (V.O.)

Now I see.

The kindness... it has a price.

The lift stops. Cooler air. Outside.

VOICE

We're here, Toby.

Toby's legs buckle. He's led to a bench.

WARDEN

He's in shock. Give him space. I'll introduce him.

Applause breaks out as the blindfold is removed. Toby blinks, over a thousand inmates stare back.

TOBY (to crowd)

As your Workshop Manager... I promise fairness.

Participation is voluntary, but encouraged.

This is the largest prison Workshop in the U.S., right here in Melbourne. Funded by America.

They want to *emulate* our Warden's model. We have the chance to lead the world.

Let's be proud. Let's show them how it's done.

The crowd erupts in applause. Over a hundred officers join in. Toby trembles. Sits back down.

WARDEN (sitting beside him) Toby, may I shake your hand? That speech... I'm proud.

You've got a criminal mind, but a business mind too. You're here for life. No parole.

So, build something that makes you happy. There *may* be privileges ahead.

Toby nods slowly. The applause still ringing in his ears.

PRISON INTERROGATION ROOM

WARDEN (firmly):

I must ask you, Toby… I was observing you earlier. You scanned the prisoners as you spoke. Paused a few times when your eyes met theirs. Do you know some of them?

TOBY (calmly):

Yes, Sir. I do. We've worked the streets of Melbourne together. Gangs formed in the old days… criminals poached to join emerging crews.

WARDEN:

Then they must have recognized you too?

TOBY (nodding):

Oh, that's for sure. Names may fade, but faces, never. Faces of allies... and enemies.

On the outside, survival has corners to hide in. Inside here? You're exposed. No hiding, just risk.

To survive inside, you pay. A lot.

PRISON MAZE – LATER

Privately, the Warden leads Toby through the prison. This time, Toby is not blindfolded. The Warden's keys rattle as they unlock door after door. Toby shuffles along in shackles.

A different path is taken, still ground level. The lift from before is gone.

They stop. The Warden grabs Toby's shackled hands, stares him dead in the eyes.

WARDEN (pointed):

I asked about those men earlier. I knew you knew them.

You see, Toby... I have degrees in Psychology. Behavioral science, to be exact. They don't hire dummies to run this place.

Toby reads the signal loud and clear.

TOBY (clearing throat):

Of course not, Sir. I'd never suggest otherwise.

Toby's eyes begin to well. The Warden sees more than words.

WARDEN:

Something's bothering you, Toby. Out with it.

TOBY (voice low):

Clarity puts me in danger. You were right, your observations were spot on. Some of those men... I've wronged them.

Killed their brothers. Their wives. Revenge is always on the menu when you live this life.

If they join the program, I'll be working side by side with them in the Workshop. Perfect place for payback.

A pause.

TOBY (continuing):

There had to be nearly a thousand men in there today. Rebellion's brewing. You've read my court transcripts, haven't you?

WARDEN (stern):

Yes, I have. Did you think you were heading to a picnic when they loaded you into that van?

You built this 'Trio' thing. You brought death, ruined families. Retribution was inevitable, Toby. It's fact. You'll have to face it.

EXERCISE YARD – MOMENTS LATER WARDEN:

Look to your right, Toby. What do you see?

TOBY (stunned):

That's… enormous. What is it?

WARDEN (chuckles):

That, my friend, is *your* building. That's *The Workshop*.

TOBY:

Stone the flaming crows...

WARDEN:

Yes, Toby. You're going to oversee it.

TOBY:

I'm absolutely amazed. You said I'd see it today. Let's check it out.

The Warden fumbles with his keyring, finds the right one, and opens the massive door.

WARDEN:

Here we go. We're in.

TOBY (stepping inside, looking around):

I could do a lot with this. Challenging, sure—but I give you, my word.

WARDEN (smiling):

That's what I wanted to hear.

WORKSHOP COMPLEX – CONTINUOUS

They walk through. Toby is in awe. Fully equipped kitchens, massive dining hall, showers, restrooms, restaurant-style furnishings.

TOBY:

This Hall… it's six times larger than ours.

WARDEN:

Plenty of planning went into this. Are you up for the challenge?

TOBY (nodding):

Oh yes. To be called the manager of this? Breathtaking.

PORCH, SOUTHERN END OF BUILDING – MOMENTS LATER

Two large wingback chairs sit in front of a circular dining table.

WARDEN:

Take a seat, Toby. Let's relax a moment.

The Warden pulls out his phone, makes a hushed call.

A sound echoes nearby, rattling plates and cutlery. A trolley is pushed toward them. Behind it, three officers, the "Boys", grinning.

TOBY (surprised):

Oh, my goodness… It's the officers!

OFFICERS (in unison):

Congratulations, Mr. Manager. The Chef welcomes you to the new complex.

The trolley holds sandwiches, pastries, coffee, and tea. Toby blushes, crimson red, slightly embarrassed.

TOBY:

Wow… what a wonderful thing to do.

WARDEN (with a grin):

This is the beginning of an *Empire*. Just like the 'Trio' you built.

Toby's face turns from crimson to suffocating red. The officers pull up chairs. As they enjoy the food...

OFFICER:

Warden, we've done what you asked. In an hour, reps from hardware stores will meet us in the Dining Hall. Catalogues ready. Toby will choose what's needed.

WARDEN:

Toby, you'll have access to the latest tech. Building materials. Tools. Everything.

OFFICER:

We estimate about a thousand inmates may join the program. Plan accordingly.

TOBY (assured):

I've thought this through. I've got it covered.

After all, I'm used to spending other people's money.

That's why there's *billions* of dollars in treasure chests back at the mansion

Realization hits, he's said too much. A fatal ego slip. The Warden and officers exchange knowing glances.

BATHROOM – MOMENTS LATER

An officer escorts Toby to the restroom.

Back on the porch, Warden and two officers exchange hushed words.

WARDEN (cold):

That bastard has billions stashed away. His ego gave him up. He was always too big for his boots. Now his mouth proves it.

He turns deadly serious.

WARDEN (commanding):

Not. One. Word.

If either of you breathes this to anyone, I'll personally bury you in the prison graveyard. Got it?

OFFICERS:

Yes, Sir.

WARDEN:

Tell the officer with Toby, but only when you're alone.

And remind him, there are plenty of graves. The Monks dug them. Dumb bastards. They dug their own too, working for Toby.

He leans in.

WARDEN (gritting his teeth):

Toby fears retribution from the inmates? He hasn't seen *anything* yet.

Retribution is coming, from new sources. And it will be *deadly*.

DINING HALL – LATER

Toby returns. The Warden takes control.

WARDEN:

Time's up. Let's head to the Dining Hall. Hardware reps are waiting.

They enter. Toby is led to the head of the table and sits. A doorbell rings.

The Warden greets the consultants, leading them in with a fake smile.

WARDEN:

Gentlemen, meet the officers. And this, *is Toby*. He's the new Manager of the Workshop Facility.

The consultants extend hands, but pause, they realize Toby is shackled. They nod instead.

Catalogues are spread across the table, duplicates for all.

WARDEN:

Toby will lead the order placements. This is his responsibility.

CONSULTANT:

Mr. Toby, help us understand what you propose for the facility. Tell us what you need, and we'll deliver.

Chapter Twenty-Two
❧The Henchman in Detention❧

The pungent odor of failure consumes Augustus.

His loyalty to Toby and Marguerite, joining forces to become a 'Trio' of fortune, has led to nothing. Behind prison walls, karma reigns. The dead at his hand will never set him free. Guilt will consume him too.

Guilt sits in the pit of the stomach, gnawing at the brain. A conscious bitterness that burns within, sour as lemons. It is a destructive force, unrelenting, a fatal blow to the psyche. This will never set Augustus free. It will niggle, bite, tear at him, shredding his being.

Multiple prison vans arrive at the mansion to collect Augustus and the Truck Drivers. They are the last villains to be removed from society, a moment celebrated by the tormented residents who've endured so much. The criminals are transported to the Farnsworth Melbourne Detention Facility, a maximum-security prison for the most heinous offenders. It is as close to Hell as Augustus and his crew will ever be.

The rotten will rots. The gates of Hell beckon. The furnace heat awaits. The Devil is watching.

In the tapestry of Augustus's life, his future had already been woven. A path carved in ruin, a dismal, pathetic ride to nowhere. The taste of failure lingers. The punch of dark gloom still lands. Burning candles of sorrow flash in his mind.

His mother's anguish appears to him every night when he closes his eyes. Sleepless nights gnaw at him. Audrey, his mother, perished in her own home. Her obsession with burning candles, her comfort, became her demise. One night, she fell asleep with them still lit. The house burned down. Trapped and alone, she died. The cruel irony, candles she adored ended her life.

These memories haunt Augustus in his restless sleep. It's been nearly fifteen years, but he still feels the heat. Still smells the smoke. Still dreams of his mother's final scream.

Yet there lies a deeper irony. Augustus mourns his mother, yet showed no remorse as he brought death to strangers. He destroyed families, shredded communities, and for what? Power. The kind of man who grieves his mother but shows no regret for his victims is no man at all.

There is no closure for the victims' families. No justification. His grief may be real, but society owes him no sympathy. His crimes were deliberate. Calculated.

Ruthless. If there is guilt, it came too late.

Now incarcerated, *The Henchman in Detention* begins his life sentence. Deservedly so.

The gates of Hell await him.

Foolish decisions led him down a path of no return. His spirit, splintered. His body, broken. His soul, wasted. No sympathy earned.

Burn in Hell, you bastard.

Crime does not pay. The ghosts of Augustus's past, those he killed, gnaw at him. Nibble by nibble, chunk by chunk, until nothing remains but an empty shell.

In contemplation, he whispers:

In the end, I will become a ghost. Just like the ones in the mansion. The ones who drifted room to room when guests arrived.

Now, *I* am the ghost.

Trapped behind a different kind of wall. A prison wall.

For life.

The thought is killing me. That is the price I must pay.

I'm just grateful my mother Audrey is not here to see this. She's in Heaven.

A place I'll never see.

The only familiar faces in prison are the truck drivers, my old crew, but even they feel distant. The past might catch up in the form of other inmates too. I've made enemies. Many.

Toby. Marguerite. The thrill we had as a trio is gone. I

once felt powerful. They called me *The Henchman*. My name alone brought fear. Now? I'm nothing. I fear the ghosts I saw in that mansion will return. I fear my own mistakes more.

Forgiveness? That's a foreign concept to me. I don't know how to seek it.

My anxiety is ramping. Peaking. I'm bewildered. For the first time in my life… I don't know what to do.

I wish my dear mother Audrey was here. There I go again, looking for a scapegoat.

A shadow appears at the cell door. A voice echoes, deep, harsh, commanding: "Stand before me, Henchman."

Augustus stands.

The Governor enters. "My name is Boris."

Tall. Jet black hair. Piercing brown eyes. Stocky like a quarterback. Augustus, though large himself, feels dwarfed. Boris crosses his arms, a picture of authoritarian power. A silent challenge. Augustus puffs his chest, widens his stance. He knows intimidation. He's used it. Learned it in the military.

But Boris clenches his fists. Pure strength. Augustus's legs tremble. He tries to hide it.

Six prison officers appear from nowhere, splitting into formation, three on each side of the Governor. Perfect symmetry. Like a military march. A show of power.

Augustus freezes. Intimidated. Defeated.

Shoulders slump.

Eyes locked on the Governor's chiseled chin and burning stare.

The cell door slides open. The guards march in. On the count of three, they stamp behind Augustus.

Intimidation tactics. Flawless.

Augustus's hands are bound with metal ties and cuffs. He's thrown to the floor. "Drag him to my office. Now," Boris growls.

They drag Augustus. No mercy. No pause. Once at the office, he's slammed against the steel door.

"Leave him," Boris orders.

"I'll deal with him when I'm ready."

The Governor and his officers step inside. The door slams shut, loud, final, symbolic.

Augustus slumps. The wall no longer supports him. He listens, but hears nothing. The door is triple-reinforced, fireproof, bulletproof. Silence.

An hour passes. It feels like ten. Then, the door clicks. Opens.

Officers grab Augustus, drag him in, slam him face-first into a steel wall. Once. Twice. Again.

His legs give way. His body slumps. Dazed. Concussed.

A wingback chair is dragged into position, a classic interrogation technique. The spotlight. The pressure point.

Augustus is hauled up, strapped in. Upright. Weak. Drenched in sweat.

Governor Boris circles him. A shark eyeing its prey. Then stops, right in front. Forces Augustus's legs open with his boots. Leans in.

Thick index finger pressing hard on Augustus's forehead. Tilts his head back.

"You belong to me now," the Governor growls. "You'll do everything I say. Is that understood?"

Augustus shakes.

The Henchman, shaking.

He's never known fear like this.

But he nods. He's met his match.

Everything he built, his empire, is gone. The streets ruled by others now. The money is useless. Inaccessible. He and the trio are broken.

Worse still, he's now ruled by *them*. The prison elite. The Governor and his officers. And they may be killers too.

"You're rubbish," Boris sneers. "And what do I do with rubbish? I dispose of it. But not yet."

He picks up the phone. "Now," he says.

Officers surround Augustus. Shackles removed. He squirms—too late. A straightjacket is retrieved and fastened around him.

The Governor claps.

"I like this look," he chuckles. "Defenseless. Perfect."

Augustus seethes. Rage boils in his veins. He dreams of strangling the Governor. Burying him in the prison yard.

But he can't move. Can't fight. Not yet.

He needs allies. He needs time.

This will become his mission:

Take the bastard out. For good. There's a knock at the door.

The Governor ambles over, opens it.

"Nice to see you again," he says. "Please… come in." Augustus turns to look

It was the bloody Judge. Yes, the Judge, Edward Vernon Blake, the bastard who sentenced us to life in prison. He smirked and said, "Hello, Henchman. Don't you recognize me? It's me, the Judge. I just popped by to see how you're getting along."

One of the truck drivers, Antonio, leaned in and whispered, "How the hell did the Judge get the Grandfather Clock from the mansion?"

"Exactly," I replied, the same thought gnawing at me the moment I saw it. The Judge must've gone back to the mansion, snooping around. He probably stole the clock and decided to play a prank on me. He saw that photo on the wall, a dead person dressed in a shroud with a frilled collar, and thought, why not dress up like it to scare the hell out of me? Truth be told, it worked. It scared the living daylights out of me.

But there's an ulterior motive behind all this. The Judge knows the Governor well. Best friends, it seems. That spells trouble, big trouble, for us. That's why I need muscle to take out that bloody Governor. And if that Judge dares show his face here again, I want him gone too.

I turned to the others. "Now do you understand why it's vital to get a message to Toby?"

"Got it, Augustus," they said. "Leave it with us. We'll let you know."

The breakfast bell rang, and the prison officers moved in to usher inmates from the dining hall back to their cells. One officer grabbed me by the neck. "I'll escort you personally," he growled. I'd never seen him before, a towering, gorilla-like figure. "No time for small talk," he said. "I'm on loan from Pentridge Prison. We'll get to know each other well during my stay."

My cell door slid open, and he shoved me to the floor. "I'll be seeing a lot of you sooner than you think," he sneered. "Oh, and I'm doing night shifts, late ones.

They can be lonely, but I'm sure you'll keep me company. Maybe give me a cuddle to soothe me… or something more intimate. See you later. And don't have a wonderful day. We don't like happy prisoners. We make them miserable at all costs."

I crawled to my bed, gripping the frame to pull myself up, exhausted and in pain. Pentridge Prison echoed in my mind. Why was this gorilla officer on loan from there? There's more to it. I'd bet the Governor's behind it. No smoke without fire.

I'd love to douse that man in petrol, set him ablaze, and watch him squirm. I'd kill him.

Restless and agitated, the pain from the beating intensified by the minute. My head throbbed, migraine-like, from the blow. Lying on my bed, anguish consumed me. My thoughts looped endlessly: the Governor's up to something. There's a connection between him and Judge Edward Vernon Blake, but how do they know each other? It's a mystery I need to solve. Are the dead talking? Feeding me information? The Grandfather Clock was targeted for a reason. If the Judge and Governor are conspiring against me, I'm a target. That gorilla officer from Pentridge must know about Toby, our connection, the Trio. They're fishing for information, and they'll get it by bashing me, maybe Toby too. I have to warn him. He's in grave danger.

Weary, I fell into a deep sleep. Hours later, a banging on my cell door jolted me awake. The gorilla officer was back, a truncheon in hand, slamming it against the bars, making a dreadful racket. "Hello, Mr. Henchman," he taunted. "We meet again. Just starting my night shift. Thought I'd say hello. Hope I didn't disturb you with all that banging. Let me put it another way, you're lucky it's the door I'm hitting. Could've been your head."

He smirked and walked away. A chill ran through me. I was right, this bastard's out to get me. I'll have to stick with the inmates when he's on duty. Safety in numbers. Better safe than sorry.

Sleep wouldn't come after that rude awakening. The trouble this officer was causing added to my woes. Lying in bed, staring at the ceiling, I missed Toby and Marguerite. I wondered how they were doing, probably as bad as me. Our freedoms gone, our lives changed forever, a death knell hanging over us. The pain and anguish stung like a memory from my past.

I was ten, at St. Kilda Beach with my mother, Audrey. We'd run along the water's edge, fascinated by the curling waves rolling in. Then I stepped on something, a sting shot through me, just like now. I screamed. My mother, my protector, rushed over. "What's wrong, darling?" She glanced at the sand as the wave receded, revealing blue bottles, not the glass kind, but jellyfish. Their sting is horrific, immediate. Known as man-of-war, or *Physalia physalis*, their venom, a mix of phenols and proteins, is deadly to prey but not humans. The pain worsens if untreated. My mother carried me to a lifeguard station. The attendant removed the tentacle, wrapped my foot in ice, and hours later, the pain subsided.

A tear rolled down my cheek, missing my mother. Her death still haunted me. Faintly, I heard music, an inmate's radio playing "It's a Heartache" by Bonnie Tyler. A song from my childhood, its lyrics mirroring my aching heart and body. Healing would take time. I tossed and turned, the connections between the Governor, the Judge, and now this gorilla officer swirling in my mind. Exhausted, I finally drifted off, but not for long.

The wake-up bell blared, and you had to respond fast. Ignoring it meant trouble. Early on, a guy a few cells down ignored it, and the officers hosed him with cold water from a fire hose. He never ignored it again. I stood, made my bed neatly, and waited for the cell door to open, a daily ritual. They controlled everything here. No privacy.

I needed a shower before breakfast. Grabbing my soap and toothpaste, I stood by the door, waiting for the click of the release. Then came the bellowing announcement: "Everybody up, everybody out!" Monotonous. Same shit every morning. The officers loved waking us.

In the shower block, I overheard muttering about a "special day" but couldn't catch the details. Probably someone's birthday, I thought. I'd learn soon enough it wasn't a birthday at all.

After my shower, I returned to my cell. An officer opened the door, and I changed into fresh clothes, waiting for the breakfast bell. Five minutes later, it rang, and I headed down the corridor to the dining hall. The corridors buzzed with chatter about "visitors' day." Not a birthday, visitors. I was usually solemn on these days. No one visited me, except the uninvited Governor. The inmates were upbeat, gloating about their visits at dinner.

In the dining hall, I spotted the truck drivers. They waved me over, offering a seat. "We've got good news, Henchman," they said.

"I could use some," I replied. "Had a dreadful night. New officer, looks like a gorilla, has it out for me. He's on loan from Pentridge. Spells trouble. Nothing good comes from this. I think he's a spy for the Governor."

"We've seen him," they said. "But here's the good news"

The dining hall filled with officers yelling prisoners' names, escorting them to meet visitors. Amid the commotion, the truck drivers leaned in. "We got a message to Toby. A guy's coming to visit you today. Your first visitor."

"Wow, you boys work fast," I said, grinning. "Who's the

guy?"

"Name's Larry Lovelace."

I burst out laughing. "Larry Lovelace? That's a silly name. Probably made up."

"At least it cheered you up," they said. "You seemed angry earlier."

"I was. This new officer's a bad egg. I need to take him out, and the Governor too. Maybe this Larry Lovelace is the answer."

The dining hall was quieter than usual, inmates eating quickly to meet their visitors. An officer's voice boomed, "Augustus, you have a visitor. Follow me now!"

I followed him to the meeting room, where he briefed me on the rules. "You'll be in a box with a glass panel. You're on camera the whole time. Use the phone to talk. No passing notes or paper, its contraband, and the visit ends immediately. Understood, Henchman?"

"Yes, sir," I replied.

I entered the box and saw a man sitting across the glass. I froze, profiling him. He looked uneasy, pointing at the phone. I snapped out of my daze, picked it up, and he did the same.

"Why would a prisoner be let out to visit another prisoner?" I asked skeptically. "Doesn't make sense."

"Easy to explain, Mr. Henchman," he said. "I'm Larry Lovelace, a librarian at Pentridge Prison. I deliver books and magazines to inmates, so I get special privileges. My trolley's right here, full of books. After this, I'll deliver to inmates here."

I laughed. "I know what you are, Lovelace. You're a fairy, aren't you?"

His face hardened. "Listen carefully, Henchman. I may be effeminate, but I've survived the prison system longer than you. They call me Larry Lovelace because I wear ladies' lace underwear to entertain inmates and do… favors. I know all about you too, mass murderer. Inmates are out to get you. Don't speak to me like that.

I'm here to help with your problem, the one you messaged Toby about."

My demeanor softened. "I'm sorry, Larry. I was out of line. My head's a mess, new to this place, anxiety's eating me alive."

"All forgiven," Larry said. "Let's get to it. You sent a message to Toby at Pentridge, right?"

"Yeah, through the truck drivers and some inmates here."

"It's delivered. I gave it to Toby personally. He's doing well, managing a project for Warden Brown. Now, about your message, you need to take out the 'Big Garbage,' right? I'm avoiding names, you understand."

"I know who you mean." I said. "I'm organizing muscle for that. There's another problem, a new officer from Pentridge, the Big Gorilla, giving me a hard time."

Larry laughed, and I frowned. "Not at you," he said. "That's his nickname at Pentridge, Big Gorilla."

I chuckled. "He needs to go out with the garbage too, Larry."

"Got it. I'll talk to Toby and let you know when the muscle's ready. Toby's got invitations for a 'Grand Opening' in my trolley. Pick them up in the dining hall later. Tell Toby I miss him, and I'm proud of him."

"I will," I said. "He's in a better spot than me right now."

"Toby had a rough start, like you," Larry said. "He was a target because some victims were inmates' relatives, and you're part of his team. That's why you're a target too. But leave it to me. You'll be surprised by the outcome. You'll get what you deserve."

"Thanks, Larry. Pleasure meeting you."

The visit ended. I slid the door open and froze, Officer Phillips, the Big Gorilla, stood there. "Enjoy your boyfriend's visit?" he sneered.

Before I could respond, a voice blared over the intercom: "Officer Phillips, come to my office immediately."

Phillips glared. "I must go. The Governor wants me."

I smirked. "Better not keep him waiting, Officer Phillips."

He shot me a stern look. "I'll be seeing you." Another officer escorted me back to my cell.

Walking down the corridors, I smiled. I had his name now. Let the games begin. I play to win.

Back in my cell, I started to relax, but doubt crept in. Don't count your chickens before they hatch. The war's not won; the battles are just beginning. I rested my head, drifting toward sleep, when a loud banging startled me. I sat up, staring at the bars. It was him, Officer Phillips.

"Hello, Mr. Henchman," he said as the door slid open. "I'm back to collect you for the Governor."

My blood drained, my face whiter than snow. I trembled. Not the bloody Governor, what does he want now? Phillips grabbed me by the neck, marching me down the corridors, yelling, "The Henchman's going to see the Governor, everybody!"

Inmates clamored to their doors, chanting and clapping. "The Governor's going to have his way with you, Augustus! Wish we could watch. Have a lovely time!"

At the Governor's door, Phillips slammed me to the ground and kicked my head. The door opened, and I was dragged in, dazed but recovering. Slammed onto a chair facing the Governor's desk, I froze in fear. Larry Lovelace sat next to the Governor. I glared at him, a lump in my throat.

Phillips pulled a chair in front of me, eyeballing me. "Your boyfriend's here, and he wants to show you something."

Larry stood, shedding a dressing gown I hadn't noticed. I burst into tears. He paraded around in ladies' lace underwear. I screamed, "Kill me now! I've had enough of this torture. I'd rather die than touch that freak! You're all insane!"

The Governor leaned forward. "Nice of you to speak so highly of us, Augustus. For that, you'll pay. We're not going to kill you. We're just going to teach you a lesson you'll never forget. Let's talk about your visit first."

My good friend Larry Lovelace informed me that a message was written and meant to be delivered to Toby Forsyth at Pentridge Prison. Larry was supposed to have delivered it, but alas, that was a tiny white lie, it never reached Toby. Instead, it was delivered to me. So, let me ensure I understand this correctly: it is your intention, or, to use a better phrase, to "take me out." Furthermore, you had another plan to "take out" my officer, Mr. Phillips. Well, henchman, I have news for you: that is not going to happen.

We've discussed that you should be punished for your intentions, and we have a little surprise for you. This morning, Larry told you that you're targeted for the murders of loved ones of prisoners and management. That was no lie, it's true. That's why you're in prison, my boy. You killed our loved ones, and so did Toby. His promotion to manager of the new workshop isn't a reward for those murders. Oh no, his promotion will soon become a demotion he doesn't see coming. He'll be surprised indeed.

Warden Brown at Pentridge Prison is a very good friend of mine. You see, Augustus, we're like family, and when we lose a family member, or rather, when you, Toby, and Marguerite did that, we are unforgiving. You seem to think incarceration is enough punishment for your crimes. Oh no, my dear henchman, that's not nearly enough. Society deserves more than the "Trio" simply being locked up. There must be a little discomfort along the way, that's only fair. Our good friend Judge Edward Vernon Blake also told us about the dreadful torture you inflicted on Theo's poor, innocent victims. As Governor, it would be remiss of me not to have a bit of fun at your expense.

The Governor reaches for his phone and dials a number. Augustus, listening intently, hears the words, "Send them in." That can only mean one thing: I'm going to be beaten severely again. I want to be dead. I hope they kill me today. There's a knock at the door, and the room falls eerily silent, not a sound is uttered.

The door opens, and a group of doctors and nurses walk into the office. Augustus glares in confusion. They don't look like thugs or criminals here to bash me. I was expecting prison officers. "What the hell is going on here?" Augustus yells. The Governor replies, "You'll find out soon enough, henchman." Officer Phillips grabs Augustus's arms and handcuffs him, standing behind him. "You're going to love this," Phillips says. "Just wait until the doctors and nurses do their stuff. It'll be fun."

Plastic sheets are laid on the floor, and the medical team arranges surgical instruments on the Governor's desk: scalpels, knives, electric saws. Augustus's eyes bulge with fright. Officer Phillips, still holding him, says, "See the pretty surgical tools? They're going to be used on you, free of charge. And you don't even have to pay for an anesthetist because there isn't one. We're doing this 'cold turkey,' no frills, an amputation with no fanfare. But at least, Augustus, you have all your friends cheering you on as you battle excruciating pain, just like our loved ones felt. You know what I mean."

Duct tape is bound around Augustus's mouth and head. "We must consider the noise factor for our neighbors." the Governor says. "We wouldn't want to disturb the peace, would we?" Officer Phillips throws Augustus onto the plastic sheets.

The whirl of the electric saw hums through the office. Terrifying screams emanate from Augustus, though they're faint through the duct tape. The Governor smiles with glee. Larry Lovelace frowns at Augustus. "I wore my best underwear for you, and you didn't want to touch me," Larry says. "So, I hope it hurts like hell, and you feel the agony you so richly deserve."

Augustus's body goes limp. Tourniquets are applied to both upper limbs to stop the bleeding. Both of his legs have been amputated well above the knees. He'll spend a week in the prison infirmary recovering. The Governor remarks, "Well, that was most entertaining. Larry, be sure to tell Toby that Augustus got into a brawl with other inmates and had to be hospitalized. Don't mention the amputation, I want that to be a very special surprise for Toby moving forward."

Augustus is removed from the Governor's office and taken to the prison infirmary. The Governor holds a meeting with Larry Lovelace and Officer Phillips. "Well, that was a bit of excitement for the day," he says. "Now we need to get down to business. I have great plans for us, so listen carefully. I have a few chores for both of you that must be completed. The road we're about to travel is the path to fortunes, the Yellow Brick Road. Most of the work has been done by the villainous Trio, but I need to make a few adjustments.

"First, Officer Phillips, I'm putting you in charge of a little project, one of many, in fact. Go to the infirmary and collect Augustus's amputated legs. Wrap them in cellophane and place them in a freezer for safekeeping. They're a present for Toby Forsyth, the newly appointed manager of the workshop at Pentridge Prison.

Second, you, Larry Lovelace, and Officer Phillips will head to the Mansion on the Hill after this meeting. You'll be followed by forty prison vans, the largest in the fleet. Empty the entire contents of the house and load everything into the vans.

Once loaded, the drivers will receive instructions to deliver to the loading docks of the new workshop building. All items will be stored for safekeeping until I can inspect them later. There should be a treasure trove of money and valuable jewelry. Don't even think of stealing anything. As a reminder, stand up and walk to my windows. Tell me what you see."

Larry Lovelace and Officer Phillips Walk to the window and say, "We see a graveyard."

"That's correct, gentlemen," the Governor says. "If you steal anything from the Mansion, that's where you'll end up. Do I make myself clear?"

"Yes, Governor, crystal clear, sir," they reply.

"Sit back down. We have more to discuss. We're expecting a couple of visitors shortly."

There's a knock at the Governor's door. "That'll be the visitors now, right on time," the Governor says. "I'm a stickler for punctuality, very impressive." He opens the door, and two gentlemen walk in: Warden Brown and Judge Edward Vernon Blake.

"Nice to see you again," the Governor says. "Please, come in and take a seat. I'm just conducting a meeting with my trusty fellows here, Officer Phillips and, of course, Larry Lovelace, whom you know intimately, I believe. His contribution to… sexual relief is well-documented and provides a wonderful service. I'd like to update you on what transpired here almost an hour ago. Larry reported to me after a visit this morning with 'the henchman,' Augustus. He told me a hit was being planned on you, Warden Brown, and myself. Augustus stupidly got his truck driver mates to hustle some muscle with inmates, and Toby was supposed to get the message, but that never happened. So, a little intervention was needed. I pride myself on solving problems, gentlemen, and they disappear quickly. Augustus was dealt with, I had both of his legs amputated. They'll be a gift for Toby Forsyth at the grand opening of the workshop in due course."

Warden Brown nods. "Do you agree it would be nice for your new manager to receive some recognition for his efforts?"

"I do indeed, Governor," Brown replies. "I'm pleased to hear about the henchman. I hope he suffered tremendous agony during his little operation."

"Oh, he did," the Governor says. "We were all here to witness it. It's been a splendid morning, and things can only get better. I have more exciting news to share. My boys will be clearing out the contents of the Mansion later today.

Warden Brown, can the loading docks of your new workshop accommodate large truck access?"

"That sounds like a splendid idea," Brown says. "I have plenty of storage space. Raiding the house will reap substantial rewards for all of us, I'm certain."

The Governor turns to Judge Blake. "Judge Edward, I have a little idea. I think the deed to the Mansion should be turned over to us. With your exceptional knowledge of law and a few loophole angles, I'm sure you could secure that property. From what I hear, the house is fully equipped with security, a morgue, and other facilities. We wouldn't want criminals replicating what the Trio invested in. This could be a perfect business opportunity, a wealth of immeasurable scale. The Trio made billions, and it must be stashed somewhere in that property. My men will search diligently for it over the coming months. What do you think of my proposal, Judge? I'd appreciate your expertise."

"What a splendid idea, Governor," Blake replies. "I'm sure I can work something out. I'll find the title deed and make things happen to transfer ownership to us. The house is abandoned now, with the Trio incarcerated for life, they won't be going back. It's an ingenious idea. My wife, Olga, could help with other matters. As Governess at Barwon Prison for Women, she knows Marguerite Forsyth, Toby's wife, is there. When I sentenced Marguerite, the brains of the Trio, I knew Olga would sort her out. My wife is tough as bricks; she'll make Marguerite's life a living hell."

Blake continues, "When I went to the Mansion and stole the grandfather clock, the shroud, and the frilled collar, there were still photographs of the dead strewn across the floor. That's where I got the idea to scare Augustus. He must have wondered who broke into the house because he recognized the clock immediately.

Marguerite, with her weird obsession with photographing dead people, gave me the hint to pretend to be dead. Olga put white makeup on me, and I was very convincing as a corpse. Augustus nearly fainted when he saw me. When I spoke and said, 'Hi, Augustus, it's me, the Judge,' he nearly collapsed with fright right here in this office. That was the greatest day."

Chapter Twenty-Three
&The Mansion Heist&

Augustus awoke in the infirmary, disoriented, sore, and in excruciating pain. A nurse passing by noticed he was conscious.

"Where am I?" he asked.

"You're in the infirmary, Augustus," the nurse replied. "And from all accounts, you've been a very naughty boy."

"How did I get here?" Augustus exclaimed. "The last thing I remember, I was in the Governor's office, but I can't recall what happened."

"Well, as I said, you've been naughty. You had a visitor this morning, Larry Lovelace, and you told him you wanted to organize a hit on the Governor and Officer Phillips. That didn't go down well. Larry told the Governor, and he punished you severely. He had both your legs amputated. That's why you're here for recovery."

Augustus screamed, "That bastard Governor chopped my legs off!" He went into deep shock, screaming the ward down. The nurse injected him with a sedative to calm him and administered morphine for the pain.

As Augustus settled, he looked across the ward and saw at least twenty other men. The morphine kicked in, easing his pain. He turned to the man next to him. "What happened to you? Why are you here?"

"The Governor got me," the man replied. "He got all of us in here. Bashings happen in prisons, but we weren't bashed by inmates. We were targeted by Governor Boris. That poor bloke over there had his arm cut off with a hacksaw for threatening to kill the Governor. You can't beat the system or trust anyone here.

Honestly, I wish I was dead. I've got a life sentence, and my life isn't worth living. When I get the chance, I'll commit suicide. It's the only way out of this hellhole."

The man's words struck Augustus. "Governor Boris showed me the graveyard from his office window and said he'd put me there. That's his trump card, instill fear, and prisoners obey. Revolt, and you end up maimed, tortured, or dead. Now I have no legs, confined to a wheelchair. My life isn't worth living either. Its clear Governor Boris calls the shots, but the irony is, he and the prison system are worse than the murderers incarcerated here. Judge Edward Vernon Blake keeps this system running. He must be getting kickbacks from the Governors and Wardens. It's a money-making racket."

Meanwhile, Judge Edward Vernon Blake spoke to Governor Boris. "I have an idea."

"Do tell, Edward," Boris replied.

"Having visited the mansion before, I think we should all go together to complete your mission. My chauffeur is waiting downstairs."

"Alright," said Boris. "Give me a couple of minutes to inform my secretary. Warden Brown, care to join us?"

"Count me in," said Warden Brown. "I'd like to see this notorious place myself."

They piled into the Judge's private limousine, heading for the Mansion on the Hill.

On the way, the Judge warned, "Brace yourselves. It's not a pretty sight. I only entered the parlor, and that was frightening enough. The front door opens to an imposing staircase. When I stepped inside, the temperature plummeted. Cold air swirled around the parlor, icy cold. I thought I heard voices, but the house was empty. Clothes were discarded in a corner, and I saw an old grandfather clock and a shroud with a collar. I grabbed what I could and left. The murder trial transcripts painted a gruesome picture of what happened there. We must investigate thoroughly, leave no stone unturned, including the private graveyard the Trio built."

The chauffeur announced, "We're a couple of minutes from the mansion." As they pulled up, the group stared at the massive, imposing structure.

"It must be worth a fortune," said Governor Boris. "When Judge Edward secures the title, we'll be sitting on a gold mine. Why let this fall to another criminal syndicate? It's ours for the taking."

They stepped out, pausing at the front gate to take in the grandeur. As they approached the porch, Larry Lovelace noticed, "The front doors ajar. Could someone be inside? Squatters, maybe?"

"Good observation," said Warden Brown. "Proceed with caution."

Officer Phillips, quiet until now, spoke up. "I'm fine, not scared. I was a sniper in the Army. I've seen atrocities and dead bodies. I'm hardened. The trial transcripts and newspaper articles prepared me. I'm intrigued, though I spare a thought for the victims. The whole town's been shattered by this."

"Well said," Governor Boris replied. "Let's get inside."

As they entered the foyer, a cold snap hit them. "It's hot outside," Larry said. "You wouldn't expect the temperature to drop so drastically just inside the doorway. It's disturbing."

In the parlor, Warden Brown gasped. Photographs of dead people lined the walls, dressed as the Judge had described. Clothes lay strewn in a corner. Larry picked them up, black cloaks.

"Those belong to the Monks, members of the Trio," said Judge Edward. "They, along with truck drivers, held up a train, shot passengers, and robbed them at the Henchman's request. A brutal act against innocent civilians."

They reached the massive staircase, an eerie feeling filling the air. A foul stench, like death, permeated the room. Down a hallway, Officer Phillips shouted, "I saw something move! Come investigate!"

They arrived at double glass doors with stained-glass windows, labeled "Grand Ballroom." Phillips opened them and gasped. Dining tables were set with glassware, cutlery, and plates of rotting food. The stench was nauseating. Rats scurried from tabletops. Chairs were in disarray, suggesting a frantic escape.

Bullet holes marked the walls, and shell casings littered the floor. Judge Edward bellowed, "This is appalling! The police sergeant assured me all evidence was collected. This is sloppy work. I'll take this up with him tomorrow."

In the kitchen, chefs' knives and equipment were scattered, another sign of a hurried evacuation. Takeaway containers bore the logo of Perfection Catering Co.

The Judge noted this, recalling that two chefs were shot, per the transcripts. He resolved to contact the catering company.

Outside, in a courtyard, Warden Brown pointed to a fence. "Look closely, those wires suggest it's electrified. Touch it, and you're fried."

"You're right," said the Judge. "A chef tried to escape by climbing it and was electrocuted instantly."

Larry spotted a large shed. Thinking it might hold gardening tools, he opened the unlocked door and screamed, "There are coffins in here!"

Judge Edward was furious. "The sergeant has a lot to answer for. The investigation was supposed to be thorough. These coffins should've been removed. Still, Warden Brown, Governor Boris, these could be useful for our prison's needs."

In the shed, Officer Phillips noticed a shiny object amidst rubbish. They cleared it, revealing a treasure chest. Unlocked, it was filled with cash. Behind it, Larry found a door leading to a vault with forty more chests. "This is billions!" they exclaimed.

Governor Boris received a call, forty prison vans had arrived. He led the drivers to the shed, instructing them to load the chests first, then the house's furnishings. The operation ran smoothly, the haul estimated in the billions.

Exploring the backyard, they followed a mossy cobblestone path and stumbled upon a horrific sight: the Trio's private cemetery. Slanted headstones, splintered coffins, and intact graves dotted the area. Judge Edward was dismayed. "Forensic teams were supposed to retrieve all bodies for identification. This hasn't been done. Some coffins are empty, hopefully meaning those bodies were identified. I'll contact the police commissioner after we're done."

Bones and skeletal remains lay scattered, the stench overwhelming. "This is neglect by the police and forensic teams," said the Judge. "The disrespect to these victims is unforgivable. I believed this case was closed, but clearly, it's not."

A scream rang out. Larry Lovelace collapsed, breathless and in shock. Phillips propped him against a headstone. An exposed skeletal hand protruded from a grave. "Was this person buried alive?" Governor Boris wondered. "They tried to climb out but didn't make it."

Judge Edward agreed. "When we finish, I'm calling the sergeant and forensic teams."

The treasure chests were loaded, and the group moved to the reception room, filled with antique furniture. As drivers moved a bureau, a skeleton fell from the wall.

The drivers, shocked, demanded answers. Governor Boris apologized, urging them to continue but warning of more surprises.

Officer Phillips, reflecting on the graveyard's scale, said,

"I've seen thousands of bodies in war, but this graveyard suggests thousands more are buried here. I'll make the Henchman's life hell for this."

In the garden shed, the drivers, nervous about the coffins, were reassured by Boris to press on. The coffins were loaded into the vans.

At the grand staircase, Judge Edward paused, admiring the paintings lining the Walls, works by Da Vinci, Van Gogh, Picasso, and more. "I was wrong to say we wouldn't find art here," he admitted. "These are worth a fortune. Drivers, collect these and any others in the bedrooms."

A haze drifted across the staircase, bringing a chill. The mood shifted from euphoria to gloom. A morbid silence fell, as if something had erased their joy. Judge Edward spoke, "Life challenges us with fear and trauma. Today is one of those days. Embrace it as we move forward."

A curdling scream pierces the air, Larry Lovelace's voice. "Judge Edward, behind you! A ghostly figure of a man!" The group freezes, eyes wide. A cloudy mist swirls, chilling the air. The ghost speaks, its voice hollow: "The villainous trio, Toby, Henchman, and Marguerite, killed us. They trapped us within these walls. Please, let us out!" Judge Edward turns, but the ghost vanishes, the mist evaporating instantly.

"Everyone, settle down," Judge Edward says, steadying his voice. "I warned you we'd encounter the extraordinary.

We know murders happened here. Stick together, don't wander off. We can't afford to lose anyone. Let's keep investigating."

The group moves from the grand staircase down a dimly lit hallway lined with open doors revealing bedrooms and bathrooms. After the chilling encounter, Warden Brown halts. "Judge Edward, I need a bathroom break, urgently." The group waits, huddled together. Warden Brown enters a bathroom, closing the door for privacy. As he relieves himself, a voice echoes, distinct from the man's voice on the staircase. This one is a woman's, desperate.

"Please help me. I'm Jodie. My partner Max and I attended a cocktail party downstairs in the parlor. We heard voices from the walls, terrifying. The hosts, Toby and Marguerite, dismissed it as a prank. They led us downstairs, past what looked like prison cells. Then they ambushed us. Toby slit Max's throat with a box cutter. They killed me too." Warden Brown listens, heart pounding. "Where are you, Jodie?" he asks. "I'm trapped in the wall. Please, help me!" Finishing, he washes his hands at the basin. Reaching for a towel, he glances in the mirror and sees a woman's reflection. "Is that you, Jodie?" he whispers. "Yes, sir," she replies. "I'm a ghost. Many of us are trapped here, unable to find the light to heaven. We seek vengeance on Toby, Marguerite, and the Henchman, evil people."

"You're beautiful," Warden Brown says. Jodie's voice softens, "I was beautiful. Now I'm a skeleton, trapped for so long." A knock interrupts, someone yells, "Hurry up, Warden!" The door opens, and Jodie's reflection vanishes.

Judge Edward calls, "Are we ready to move?" Warden Brown steps out, shaken. "No, listen. I saw another ghost, Jodie. She was killed by the trio near prison cells downstairs." Judge Edward nods. "I believe you. We'll investigate downstairs soon. For now, let's check these bedrooms. Van drivers, start removing furniture, everything but the piano we'll see later."

The hallway lights flicker out. A candle glows at the corridor's end, and a ghostly figure appears. "I am Anthony Forsyth, Toby's father," it intones. "Toby and Marguerite killed me and my wife. This is our house. The dead see everything. Go to the dungeon's downstairs, you'll understand. Thousands were killed here."

Shock ripples through the group. The ghost vanishes, and

the lights return. Anthony's chilling words linger.

Music drifts from down the hall, ethereal piano notes, beautiful yet mournful. The group huddles closer, heeding Judge Edward's warning to stay together. Peering through an open door, they see a woman playing the piano. She speaks without turning: "I know you're there. I'm Betty. I play for the dead here. They were all killed in this house. My music soothes their souls." The group listens, moved by her words. Some frown, others sigh, feeling the raw emotion. Betty asks, "Shall I play for you?" Judge Edward whispers, "No, thank you. We must go." As they step back, Betty and the surrounding mist vanish, leaving a freezing blast of air.

Finding an empty room, Judge Edward calls a meeting. "Betty doesn't know she's dead," he says. "She plays for the dead, not realizing she's one of them. Do you agree?" The group nods. Larry Lovelace adds, "Her music calms the troubled ghosts." Judge Edward instructs the van drivers: "Clear this level's furniture, but leave the piano. It's Betty's solace. We'll call that room 'The Piano Room.'"

Warden Brown leads the group to a staircase beside the grand staircase, descending to a cobblestone corridor with a cold, eerie atmosphere. They reach jail cells, not like a prison, but dungeons for unwilling captives. A pungent smell, like a signature of horror, fills the air. "An injustice," Warden Brown mutters. "Vulnerable souls taken. Those villains should hang for this."

A frosted glass door looms ahead. A ghastly figure appears, holding a gift, and intones, "Welcome to Doom." The door slides open, and the figure vanishes. Inside, Larry Lovelace screams, "It's a morgue!" The temperature plummets. Freezers line the wall. Larry opens one, sliding out a tray. "See? This is for bodies." He opens another and screams, "There's a body here!" Judge Edward, furious, notes this in his book. "The sergeant assured me all bodies were removed. Another blunder!"

Voices echo from the walls. "That's my blood," says one. "I'm Bob Tucker, a coach driver. My coach broke down outside. Toby offered shelter, but we met our doom. At dinner, Bessey commented on Marguerite's strange wall pictures.

Marguerite killed her first, that's Bessey in the freezer." Judge Edward confirms, "A coach was found in a swamp nearby. Bob's telling the truth." Bob's voice adds, "The dead see everything. More bodies are in the freezers." The group opens more doors, revealing dozens of corpses.

Bob urges, "Go through those double doors to the Torture Room. It's dire." Warden Brown pushes the doors open. A foul stench hits them, blood and decay. A large bench with a circular saw dominates the room, bone splinters scattered around. Chains, whips, machetes, and axes adorn the walls. Blood splatters the ceiling. A van driver, familiar with abattoirs, compares it to cattle slaughter. Warden Brown vows, "Toby's new workshop won't compare to this, but I'll ensure he faces surprises." Judge Edward agrees, "We'll discuss this later."

Ghostly voices scream, "The trio killed us! We want revenge!" Walls crack, skeletal remains spill out, some with fresh flesh. The ghosts curse Marguerite as the mastermind. "We'll kill her first," they vow. The group feels their anguish. Warden Brown reveals, "We've dealt with Augustus, the Henchman. His legs are gone, he felt everything."

A calm settles, as if the ghosts approve. Larry Lovelace warns, "They'll return." Judge Edward agrees, "We'll ensure justice. Marguerite will face the Governess, ruthless and dangerous."

Chapter Twenty-Four
❧Olga, The Governess❧

Olga is a woman of unyielding confidence and seething anger, a combination she wears like a badge of honor. Her husband, Judge Edward Vernon-Blake, is little more than a pawn in her intricate schemes, a fallback when circumstances demand it. To Olga, her enemies are mere stepping stones, crushed underfoot by her sharp intellect and sharper resolve. She eliminates obstacles with ruthless precision, no matter the cost. Her reputation is notorious, whispered in fear among the dead prisoners who learned too late not to cross her. She is a woman not to be trifled with.

To be summoned to the office of the Governess is, for any prisoner, akin to stepping into a death trap, and often, it is. Olga's voice carries a natural menace, an accolade she cherishes. No fool, she has dealt with every kind of filth incarcerated in her prison. Her motto is simple: Flush the shit. She drills into her officers a merciless creed, show no mercy, make the inmates miserable, and she'll be watching. Send them to her, and she'll deliver misery in spades.

Tall, with sweeping locks that curl slightly, Olga's appearance deceives. Her freckled nose and sharp, wide eyes belie the predator within. Marguerite, a newcomer working on a photography project, will soon discover this. Marguerite tries cautiously to connect with the female inmates, but her efforts are met with scorn. The prisoners taunt her, sneering, "Still planning to dress us up in shrouds, bitch?" Their resentment is palpable, and Marguerite's opinions are dismissed.

Powerless, she realizes she must devise a plan to win them over quickly, or risk futility and danger.

In the dining halls, officers pin up posters advertising workshop activities: art classes, needlework, and photography. Marguerite, passing by, remarks, "I could teach you all so much about photography if you'd give me a chance." Officer Quinn nods. "Fair enough. Time to bury the hatchet, don't you think?" Laughter erupts around the table, but Helga, the Top Dog, whispers to her crew, "Yeah, a hatchet in that bitch's head, more like." Helga is a force of nature, and crossing her is akin to signing your own death warrant. Yet, she approaches Marguerite with a proposition. "Alright, bitch, let's call a truce." Marguerite extends her hand, shaking Helga's firmly. Helga leans in, her voice low. "Step out of line, and I'll kill you instantly, understand?" Marguerite nods, undeterred, but the words sear into her memory.

The workshop program gains traction across Barwon Prison's varied sections, housing inmates from petty thieves to murderers. Open to all, regardless of their crimes, the program signals a tentative peace, or so Marguerite believes. With the "hatchet buried," she secures a role teaching photography, thinking old wounds are mended. But this is a delusion. The inmates' acceptance is a facade, and a storm brews, aimed directly at her.

The workshop venue, a sprawling former warehouse east of the prison, is handpicked by Olga. Renovated under the supervision of trusted officers Quinn, Braddon, and Vera (known as "Vinegar Tits"), the space transforms into a modern hub. Equipment is installed, and a medical facility, complete with a curious "Dental Clinic" is established, a choice of Olga's that raises eyebrows among the officers. They speculate about its purpose but never question her. Olga's decisions are law.

Her selections for workshop leaders are calculated: Prisoner Watson for sewing, Stevens for knitting, Clydesdale for art, Maddon for woodwork, Frankston for metalwork, Jeffries for patchwork quilting, and Marguerite for photography. These are no random picks, they're Olga's informants, the "snitches" who trade loyalty for favor. Their roles are strategic, threads in the web Olga weaves silently.

Cunning as a vixen, she manipulates from the shadows, her husband Edward a compliant partner in their schemes. Though he's a supposed pillar of society, behind closed doors, Olga rules their marriage, clipping his wings with ease.

Together, they chase wealth and power, but something sinister may lurk beneath their polished exterior.

Olga rewards her loyal snitches with sweets and prime postings, a system greased by money and fear. Helga Schultz, built like a tank with a temper to match, oversees the inmates. Labeled a "lagger" for snitching, a prisoner might escape her wrath if the price is right. Money talks, and Helga listens.

Marguerite, naive, believes her wealth will shield her. Unbeknownst to her, her fortune has been seized, her ace reduced to a joker. The deck is stacked, and she's the punchline. She dreams of challenging not just the inmates but the prison's power structure, banking on her hidden riches. Reality will soon shatter her illusions.

Meanwhile, Olga is summoned to a meeting by Edward. At his office, she's greeted by the Governor and Warden. After pleasantries, Edward announces, "We are now proud owners of the mansion on the hill. My lawyers have secured the title." This bombshell, aimed at the "Trio" behind the mansion's dark history, will be revealed at the workshop's opening. Edward mentions a meeting with "the Sergeant," promising repercussions for his mishandled investigation.

Later, the Sergeant arrives, met with Edward's icy glare. "Your investigation was a half-arced job," Edward growls. "Bodies remain in the morgue's freezers, falling out of walls. Your reports were amateurish." Despite the Sergeant's excuses, Edward orders him and the Superintendent to return to the mansion and clean up the mess. Defeated, the Sergeant complies, calling the

Superintendent to meet him there.

At the mansion, Superintendent Alan Baxter waits, unnerved by growling noises from within. When Sergeant Thomas Ethan-Brown arrives, Baxter explodes. "What the hell have you done? The Judge roasted me!" The Sergeant admits the investigation was botched, bodies were missed, despite his team's assurances.

Baxter, furious, hears the growling again. "Something's not right," he snaps. "We need to investigate what the Judge is complaining about." The mansion holds secrets, and the truth is far from uncovered.

Chapter Twenty-Five
❧The Dead Are Talking Again❧

As Superintendent Alan Baxter and Sergeant Thomas Ethan Brown step through the creaking front door of the derelict mansion, a gust of stale air greets them. The cavernous hallway stretches before them, dominated by the grand staircase that looms upward, its faded opulence a ghostly reminder of forgotten grandeur. Both men glance toward it and freeze, gasping in unison. The heavy door slams shut behind them with a thunderous bang, as if propelled by an unseen hand. The force of it rattles the walls, sending a shiver through their bones. Fear wraps around them like a shroud, the air thick with a sense of entrapment.

On the staircase landing, the ancient grandfather clock stands sentinel, its pendulum swinging wildly, ticking with unnatural urgency. The chimes erupt, loud and discordant, filling the mansion with an eerie resonance. A foul odor creeps into the air, accompanied by a chilling breeze that seems to slither from the walls. Then, a high-pitched shriek pierces the silence, anguished, desperate, a cry for help.

Voices, faint at first, grow louder, chanting, "Go to the morgue, go to the morgue."

"Good God," Superintendent Baxter mutters, his voice trembling. "Where are those voices coming from?"

Sergeant Thomas Ethan Brown, his face pale, replies in a hoarse whisper, "From inside the walls, sir. I've heard them before, the last time I was here." His eyes widen. "The Judge was right, there must be bodies still here. This is a disaster, Superintendent."

"Lead the way, Sergeant," Baxter says, steadying himself. "You know where the morgue is."

They move cautiously, the air growing colder with each step, as if the mansion itself is exhaling frost. By the time they reach the morgue, the chill feels like icy tendrils coiling around their bodies, stealing their breath. The heavy morgue doors loom ahead, and with a collective push, they swing open. Instantly, the freezer drawers burst open, metal sliders screeching as they propel forward, revealing the pale, lifeless bodies within. Both men stagger back, gasping, their hearts pounding at the grotesque sight.

For a moment, they stand frozen, struggling to process the horror. Then the dead speak, their voices a haunting chorus: "Get us out of here, Sergeant. You left us behind. It's your fault no one came for us. Set us free so we can walk toward the light. We're trapped; we don't know how to find it."

Baxter, his voice barely steady, points to an open door on the right side of the morgue. "What's behind that, Sergeant?"

Brown shakes his head, his eyes wide. "I don't know, sir. I've never seen it open before. Last time I was here, it was sealed shut."

The voices rise again, sharp and accusing. "That's the torture room. They took us there, tortured us before the Trio killed us. Go through the doorway. See for yourselves."

With trepidation, the men step through the threshold and scream. The room is a nightmare: blood-stained walls, splattered and streaked with crimson, surround a wooden structure in the center, where a massive circular saw blade gleams menacingly. The voices whisper, "They chopped us up with that blade, like cattle to slaughter."

The walls begin to weep blood, cracks widening as skeletal remains tumble out, piling on the floor. Shrieks and wails grow deafening, pleading, "Help us! Show us the light!" Overwhelmed, Baxter and Brown flee, sprinting through the mansion, past the cursed staircase, and out the front door. They don't stop until they reach the front gate, collapsing against it, breathless and shaken.

Brown fumbles for his phone and dials the station. "We need backup, now. Bring vans, as many as you can. Hurry."

They stumble to a bench across the street, the mansion looming like a predator in the fading light. The cries of the dead still echo in their ears. Baxter nudges Brown. "Something strange is going on here, Sergeant. Beyond the house, I mean. I've got a feeling this is tied to the Governor, the Judge, the Warden, the Governess."

Brown nods grimly. "I've had the same thought, sir.

They're up to something, but what? Right now, we need to focus on getting help."

He calls Constable Hurley. "Get to the mansion immediately. Bring Constable Westerman and every officer available. We need vans, lots of them. There are bodies, Hurley. I'll explain when you get here. Just move fast."

While waiting, Brown's voice drops, heavy with guilt. "Last time I was here, I was terrified. The fear clouded my judgment, made me miss vital evidence—the bodies in the freezers, the torture room. I didn't even know it existed until today. I failed, sir."

Baxter places a hand on his shoulder. "Stop beating yourself up, Sergeant. What we saw in there would shake anyone. Even I struggled to think straight. You've got years of exemplary service. Pick yourself up and move forward."

When the police teams arrive, vans and forensic units in tow, Baxter and Brown brief them on the porch, the mansion's unrest palpable. Brown addresses the group, his voice steady but raw. "I believe we're being targeted, possibly by Judge Edward Vernon-Blake. I smell a rat, something sinister involving the prison officials. But right now, we have a job to do. The scenes inside are disturbing. Constable Westerman, you'll calm the spirits. You've done it before. The rest of you, collect everybody, document everything meticulously, and deliver them to the coroner. We can't afford mistakes."

Westerman steps forward, her presence calm amidst the

chaos. The ghosts swarm around her, their voices a cacophony of rage and sorrow. "You know who I am," she says softly. "I've spoken to you before. We're here to help you find peace. Follow me to the light."

She ascends the staircase, a foggy mist curling around her. The ghosts' screams grow muffled, confused. At the landing, she pauses, raising her hand toward a large window where a beam of light begins to glow, growing brighter. "You're almost there," she urges. "Keep walking." The ghosts mutter, "We see it," and with a final gasp, the mist dissipates. Silence falls, tranquil and profound.

The team erupts in applause. "Well done, Westerman!" they shout. "You walked them to the light!"

Geared up in protective suits, the officers spread out, scouring the mansion. The scene is worse than imagined, cracks in the walls wider, skeletal remains spilling out in torrents. Body bags pile up, the scale of the tragedy incomprehensible.

Amanda, the forensic chief, calls Brown to the parlor. "Sergeant, the wider cracks are significant. The bodies were hidden in the walls last time, revealed now by expansion and contraction from heat and cold. Judge Vernon-Blake saw these bodies and blamed you for an incomplete investigation. The freezers and the torture room were oversights, but the walls' physics explain the rest. I'll draft a report to back you up. And Sergeant? The only way to account for all the bodies is to demolish every wall."

Brown nods, grateful. "That would help, Amanda. If the Judge doesn't agree to demolition, the true body count will remain unknown."

Outside, Constables Hurley and Westerman tally the body bags loaded into vans, noticing unusual traffic circling the street. Hurley calls Thomas Brown. "Sergeant, we're being watched. Same vehicles, looping repeatedly."

Brown observes, then dials Judge Vernon-Blake. "Judge, we're being surveilled. Know anything about it?"

"Surveillance? No, Sergeant, I didn't arrange that. How's the investigation progressing?"

Brown explains Amanda's findings, suggesting demolition. The Judge dismisses it, advising him to deliver the bodies to Coroner Michael Stanford. Baffled, Brown shares the conversation with Amanda, noting the Judge's reluctance. "It's odd, Amanda. Why wouldn't he want the walls torn down?"

"Strange indeed," she replies.

Brown receives a call from Stanford. "Sergeant, how many bodies are coming? When?"

"At least a couple hundred, Michael. They're on their way now. It's a massive operation."

The team, hardened yet shaken, grapples with the investigation's scale. Brown reflects: "This is the worst crime scene I've ever seen. The depravity of Marguerite

Forsyth, preserving victims' suffering as trophies, it's sickening. She'll die in prison, and I hope it's with the pain she inflicted. Justice feels hollow when they're fed and housed while their victims suffered unimaginable horrors. If this were up to the public, they'd be on death row."

The mansion's secrets, exposed yet incomplete, leave a bitter weight on the team, their duty to the dead driving them forward amidst the shadows of corruption and conspiracy.

Chapter Twenty-Six

❧Opening Day Women's Workshop❧

T he atmosphere in the prison was electric, but it needed leveling. Marguerite was spiraling, her arrogance unchecked. She called the other inmates wannabe superstar criminals, but to her, they were just wankers. "I'm no wannabe," she muttered to herself. "I'm a criminal mastermind." To her, the others were amateurs, stepping on her turf. "These bitches better watch themselves. They're not gangsters. I built an empire of gangsters. Murderers? Sure. Challengers to me? Never."

Marguerite's latest stunt was stealing buy-ups from the inmates, a bold move that took time to trace back to her. When the women realized she was the culprit, they banded together and reported her to Top-Dog Helga Shults. Helga's temper rivaled Marguerite's, but she was no hothead. Known in some circles as the "Silent Assassin," Helga was calculated, her actions deliberate. Slow and steady, she believed, won the race. Her cautious, well-planned approach had earned her the title of Top-Dog, and the headstones in the prison cemetery were proof of her ruthlessness.

At dawn, the inmates were herded against the wall for roll call. Marguerite stood among them; her sniggering barely concealed. The corridors buzzed with chatter as they waited for a prison officer, or "Screw," as the inmates called them. Helga listened closely to the women's complaints, confirming their accusations against Marguerite. It was time to act.

Officer Beryl Quinn slithered around the corner like a snake, her presence startling the group. "What's all this chattering?" she bellowed. "Shut your mouths and listen, or I'll put you all on report. You'll be explaining yourselves to the Governess. Got it?"

"Yes, ma'am," the inmates muttered.

"That's better. Loosen up, there's work to be done." Quinn assigned jobs, pausing as she reached Marguerite. She locked eyes with her. "And you, *Bitch*, you're mopping the floors. I want to see my reflection when you're done. Understand?"

"Yes, ma'am," Marguerite replied.

"What did you call me, *Bitch*? Madam?" Quinn snapped, slapping Marguerite hard across the face. "Call me ma'am, not madam. Clear?"

"Clear as mud, ma'am," Marguerite said, her tone defiant.

Quinn leaned in. "I know all about you, *Bitch*. I'll be watching you. One step out of line, and you'll wish you were never born. I'll make your life hell. And that big butch Helga over there? She's my eyes and ears when I'm not around. Tread carefully."

Later, Marguerite mopped in a corner, her head down, avoiding attention. But the women had other plans. They ambushed her, tearing at her clothes until she was naked. Outnumbered, she couldn't fight back. Two inmates pinned her down, rolling her onto her stomach. Helga loomed over her. "I'm right behind you, *Bitch*," she snarled. Two others forced Marguerite's head down, arching her backside upward. Helga grabbed the mop handle and shoved it into Marguerite's anal cavity. Marguerite screamed, thrashing in agony, but no one helped. Helga pushed harder, blood spraying across the floor. The women fled, leaving Marguerite in a pool of blood, defenseless and writhing in pain.

Quinn appeared around another corner. "Sleeping on the job, *Bitch*?" she mocked from a distance. As she approached, she saw the blood and the mop handle protruding from Marguerite. Her laughter erupted, uncontrollable. Sitting beside Marguerite, she taunted, "Oh, I see Top-Dog got to you with a little help from her friends. What a mess, all that blood on your nice clean floor. That must piss you off, huh, *Bitch*? Let's just sit and chat. Can't move with that mop up your rear, can you? So, what do you do for fun around here? Not many friends, I bet."

Marguerite, in excruciating pain, begged for help. "Well, since you asked so nicely," Quinn sneered. She grabbed Marguerite by the hair and dragged her down the corridor toward the infirmary. Marguerite screamed; the pain unbearable. "Not far now, *Bitch*. Stop the noise, you're giving me a headache," Quinn snapped.

At the infirmary, a nurse chuckled. "Surprised you haven't visited us sooner. Thought the girls would've beaten you up by now. Let me guess, you pulled your panties down looking for fun? Wow, is that a mop handle in your arse? You're a little kinky, aren't you?"

Marguerite's mind raced. *These bitches in the infirmary are as crooked as the officers. They're all in cahoots. It's not what you know, it's who you know.* She saw Helga as a smaller version of herself, cunning but not invincible. *What she did with that mop handle is seared into my brain. I'll never forgive or forget. I'm a warrior, and I'll show that so-called Top-Dog who's boss.*

The doctor examined Marguerite. The bleeding had subsided, but the mop handle had caused severe damage. "You'll need stitches," he said. "The anal cavity is split. We'll attach a colostomy bag to manage waste, as you won't be able to do so normally." Furious, Marguerite vowed revenge. The doctor left her with the nurse, who would handle the sutures. "You'll be here a week or so," he added. "Protocols must be followed."

As the nurse prepared, she giggled, then burst into laughter. She called Quinn over, pulling her out of Marguerite's earshot. "I'm stitching her arse without anesthetic," the nurse whispered. "She'll feel every hook." Quinn roared with laughter. "I need you to strap her face-down and gag her," the nurse said. "She'll scream like hell."

Quinn grinned. "Can I watch?"

"Yep, this'll be fun," the nurse replied.

Quinn strapped Marguerite to the bed, binding her mouth with masking tape. "I hate you, *Bitch*," she hissed. "You killed my cousin on that train. She was about to be married, but you ruined that. I'm getting justice for all the women you've hurt." The nurse leaned in. "I'm going to make your arse feel like it's on fire. You'll wish you were dead."

The nurse stabbed the hooked needle into Marguerite's buttocks, scraping and drawing blood. She stitched slowly, pulling the thread for maximum pain.

Marguerite's tears flowed, her body rigid with agony. Quinn clapped with each stitch, laughing. "This is joyous, thrilling! Not enjoying yourself, Marguerite? Oh, silly me, you're gagged. What a shame."

The nurse taunted, "I'll tell everyone how brave you were. And here's a secret: my friend at the men's prison met your pal Augustus, 'The Henchman.' She amputated both his legs, no anesthetic. Blood spurted everywhere as the saw cut through. He's in a wheelchair now, hated by the inmates, just like you. You're lucky this is all you're getting."

Marguerite was moved to a ward, heavily sedated. She woke slowly, disoriented, in a quiet corner. A new nurse, Frankston, approached. "Good morning," she said kindly. "You've had a severe operation. Take these painkillers."

Marguerite swallowed them with water. "Tea or coffee?" Frankston asked. "Coffee, please," Marguerite replied.

Looking out the window, Marguerite saw a magnolia tree swaying, its sweet aroma drifting in. She felt a rare calm. Frankston returned with coffee. "The doctor will visit after breakfast. How are you feeling?"

"Comfortable, thanks to the painkillers," Marguerite said.

Resting, Marguerite reflected on her fall from power. Once free to rule her empire, she was now confined, controlled by rules she despised. Her thoughts turned to Augustus, now wheelchair-bound. *A man feared, now living in fear.*

Weeks later, Marguerite was recovering. A surprise visitor arrived: Officer Vera, nicknamed "Vinegar Tits."

"I'm coordinating the Women's Workshop," Vera said. "I think you should take charge. You're a strong businesswoman with organizational skills. What do you think?"

Marguerite hesitated. "I'm a target. The women attacked me, that's why I'm here."

"Attacks happen," Vera shrugged. "It's prison. You'll overcome this. The workshop is ready. I need your confirmation to lead it."

"I'll think about it," Marguerite said.

Days later, Vera returned. "Good news, you're cleared to leave the infirmary. Have you decided?"

"I have doubts," Marguerite admitted. "The women want revenge. How can I be safe?"

"I've spoken to them," Vera assured her. "They know you're ill and to back off. Will you take the role?"

"Yes, if you can protect me," Marguerite agreed.

Vera escorted Marguerite to her cell, then suggested, "Let's drop your things off and tour the workshop."

"Sounds awesome," Marguerite replied.

"When it's just us, call me Vera," she said. "But around others, it's Officer Vera. No favoritism."

At the workshop, Marguerite gasped. The space was stunning, with sewing machines, metalworking tools, and a canteen. Spotting machetes on a bench, she thought, *I can use those if needed.* Vera, overcome, kissed Marguerite briefly.

Playing along, Marguerite sighed, "That was sweet." She kissed Vera back, more intensely, cementing her ally.

The workshop included a medical center and dentist, which Marguerite found odd. "It's for accidents," Vera explained. "The Governess insisted."

Monday arrived, opening day. Marguerite organized paints, fabrics, and tools. Officers Quinn, Briggs, Wheatley,

Braddon, and Vera praised her setup. "The Governess sends her best," they said. "You're the manager now."

Inmates streamed in, and Marguerite gave a welcome speech. To everyone's surprise, the women clapped sparingly. She unveiled photography equipment, sobbing with joy. Snapping photos, she felt alive, a contrast to her infamous corpse photography.

But trouble brewed. At lunch, Helga muttered, "I smell a rat. Marguerite's crawling up the Screws' arses. She's got them wrapped around her finger. I'll teach her a lesson."

Later, Helga taunted Marguerite about Augustus. Enraged, Marguerite grabbed a machete, hiding it in her overalls. Approaching Helga, she struck, slicing off her head. In a frenzy, she beheaded the women who had assaulted her. Screams erupted. Officer Braddon locked the doors. The officers subdued Marguerite, and Quinn sedated her. "She's going to the Hole," Quinn said.

Briggs called the Governess, Olga, who was meeting her husband, Judge Edward- Vernon-Blake, Warden Brown, and Governor Boris. They had secured the deed to Marguerite's mansion. The Judge warned, "Keep this quiet. No police. We're the Quad now, and this mansion is our ticket to the criminal world."

Olga returned to the prison, ordering Briggs to throw Marguerite in solitary. "There are severed heads everywhere," Briggs reported. "Helga's dead. The inmates are freaked out."

Chapter Twenty-Seven
❧The Visit to the Dentist☙

The Governess arrived back at the prison. She called Briggs.

"I want all my officers, even the ones not on duty. I want them here immediately. Tell them the Governess has called an urgent meeting. They are to report to my office without delay. For now, I'll meet you and the others in the Workshop. I'm on my way. Stay calm and in control."

Moments later, she entered the Workshop. Her loyal officers, those on shift, met her at the front doors.

"Hello, Governess," Briggs greeted her.

"Before we go inside," Briggs continued, "let's head to the meeting room for a chant. We'll explain everything that happened today. Then we'll show you the bodies, the dead ones. They're still lying on the floor."

"Okay, ladies. That sounds like a good idea," said the Governess. "Let's talk."

She paused. "First things first... Where's that bitch Marguerite?"

"We dragged her down by the hair," one officer said. "She fought us, even though she was sedated. She put up a hell of a fight. We beat the hell out of her. Probably broke a couple of ribs too."

"That's the least of her worries," muttered the Governess. "She'll get worse when I get my hands on her."

Inside the meeting room, the officers recounted the day.

"It was going fine. The prisoners were engaged in activities. Marguerite was surprisingly good with them, communicative, calm. We had lunch. It was orderly. Afterward, Top Dog Helga taunted Marguerite. Credit where it's due, Marguerite walked away."

"What did Helga say?" the Governess asked.

"She told Marguerite that Augustus, the Henchman, had been 'cut down to size.' Literally. That his legs had been chopped off."

The Governess's face darkened.

"So, Marguerite walked away, but she was clearly shaken," another officer added. "Then she came back with a machete. She sliced Helga's head clean off."

"She also went after a group of women," another officer said quietly. "The ones who raped her when she first arrived. That happened in the showers after induction."

"She'd been biding her time," said Briggs. "We all think she wanted the Top Dog position. But Helga mouthed off at the wrong time. Marguerite saw her chance and took it."

"Enough," the Governess said. "Take me to the scene. I want to see it myself."

They walked her through the aftermath.

"What a bloody mess," she muttered. "Literally. We're going to clean this up, quietly. No police. These bodies go to the graveyard immediately. No one breathes a word of this."

She turned. "Let's head back to my office. The off-duty officers should be waiting."

Back at her office, the Governess stood before her full staff.

"Give me a moment to compose myself," she said. Then, "First, I want to thank the team that endured today's ordeal. It must have been traumatic. I saw the aftermath. And I can say this with certainty; Marguerite is a psychopath."

She took a deep breath.

"I'll reveal later what I've planned for her. But first, we need to be absolutely clear, this stays in-house. No one speaks of this. Not even among yourselves. Walls have ears. Gossip will not be tolerated. Understood?"

"Yes, Governess," they chorused.

"Oh, and no police. No press."

The Governess's voice dropped.

"You all know what that bitch has done. She's hurt people in our community. Some of you have lost loved ones because of her. It's time for justice. Here's the plan."

She paused for effect.

"We're taking her to the medical centre. To the dentist, to be specific. He's going to pull every tooth from her mouth. Then someone will cut out her tongue. She'll never speak again. She'll be mute. Finished."

The room was silent.

"Who volunteers to bring her to me in shackles?"

Officers Quinn, Wheatley, Braddon, and Briggs raised their hands.

"Good. Bring the bitch."

Half an hour later, a knock sounded at the office door.

"Come in," barked the Governess.

Marguerite was shackled. Battered. Bruised. Broken.

"Sit her on the floor," the Governess ordered. "Everyone, gather round."

Marguerite was thrown down. The Governess grabbed a chair, sat before her, and locked eyes.

"You filthy scum bitch," she hissed. "I'm going to teach you a lesson like no other. I am the boss. Not you. You've brought grief to this prison and this community. And now, revenge is ours."

She leaned closer.

"Remember when someone shoved a mop handle up your arse? You needed surgery. No anaesthetic. My nurse stitched you up raw. But that was child's play compared to what's coming."

She stood and paced.

"How do you think your victims felt? The ones you tortured? Can you imagine it? You will. You'll feel every ounce of it."

The Governess smirked.

"And yes, Augustus? It's true. Both legs. Gone. No anaesthetic. Screamed like a baby. Now it's your turn."

Marguerite was thrown into a prison van. Officers Quinn, Wheatley, and Briggs joined her in the back.

They taunted her, slapping her, banging her head into the van's walls.

"What's the matter, bitch? Feeling giddy? Say your prayers."

Briggs shouted, "Turn on the phones! Record everything. This is history."

They recorded every word.

"You're going to die in this prison, bitch."

Marguerite finally snapped.

"You're all a bunch of bitches! Every one of you is gay! Just like the inmates! Vinegar Tits kissed me this morning!"

"Who the hell is Vinegar Tits?" Briggs asked.

"That's what we call Officer Vera," Marguerite sneered. "She's got the hots for me. Told me so this morning."

Briggs narrowed her eyes. "You blew your last chance, Marguerite."

"And I bet that Governess is gay too. She sure looks like it."

"Well, let me tell you something," Briggs said. "The Governess is *not* gay. She's married, to Judge Edward-Vernon-Blake. Ring any bells?"

Marguerite froze. The silence was chilling.

The van pulled up. Briggs turned to the others.

"Leave her in there. Come with me. Under the tree."

Briggs pulled out her phone.

"I'm calling Vera. She needs to hear this recording."

They agreed. Briggs dialled.

"Vera, it's me. We're meeting in front of the dentist's office. Come now. Urgent."

Vera arrived and hugged Briggs.

"Before we go inside, listen to this," Briggs said. "It's what Marguerite said in the van."

They sat. Briggs played the recording.

Vera listened; head bowed, ashamed, embarrassed.

When it ended, she was silent.

Briggs wrapped her in a hug.

"We're mates. That doesn't change. You're a great officer."

"I froze," Vera said. "I didn't help because... I'd never seen someone beheaded before. I was in shock."

"Thank you for being honest," said Briggs. "Now... the meeting upstairs, it's judgement day for Marguerite. The Governess is furious. The plan is to take out her teeth... then her tongue."

Vera stood.

"I want to be the one to cut her tongue out. She betrayed me. She used me. I kissed her and told her it was our secret. But she was just playing me."

Briggs nodded. "Let's go talk to the Governess. We'll play her the recording."

Inside, the Governess greeted Vera with a smile.

Briggs interrupted. "Governess, may I speak with you in the hallway?"

Once outside, she explained everything, the taunting, the recording, the insults.

"She called us all gay. Said *you* were gay. We recorded it. You should hear it."

Briggs played the recording.

The Governess listened, stone-faced. When it reached the part about Vera kissing Marguerite, her expression shifted.

"That was a lack of judgment, Vera," she said. "I don't care about your orientation. But Marguerite used you. She manipulated you."

"Yes," Vera said quietly. "She used me. And I want to be the one who finishes this."

Chapter Twenty-Eight

❧The Grand Opening Men's Workshop❧

It's a crisp autumn day, with sunny skies prevailing, a momentous occasion in the history of the nation's prisons. Today marks the "New Dawning" of prison management, a bold plan of integration, unity, and a growing demand for equality. This new-age approach reflects an ever-evolving world.

Toby Forsyth, the newly appointed manager of the workshop, walks with a spring in his step, excitement pulsing through his veins. He meets Warden Brown in his office.

"Good morning, Toby! What a splendid day it's going to be," the Warden greets him warmly. A prison officer arrives, pushing a trolley loaded with croissants and coffee, placing it beside Toby before leaving.

"Please, help yourself, Toby. You need some sustenance, so dive right in," the Warden insists. Politely, Toby pours a cup of coffee and prepares a plate of croissants, not for himself, but for Warden Brown, placing them on his desk.

"Oh, that's such a kind gesture, Toby. Thank you," the Warden says, smiling. Toby then pours himself a coffee and settles into his chair.

"I'm so pleased we have this time together," Warden Brown continues. "I have important news to share. This is hot off the press: we're hosting visitors from several prisons today for the grand opening of your workshop. Pentridge must set the example as the best prison facility in the country, and I have every confidence in you, Toby, to show everyone how exceptional we are."

"Of course," Toby replies quickly. "I'm honoured to be chosen as manager, sir. Everything is in place, and all activities are ready to go."

"Splendid news, Toby!" the Warden exclaims. "We'll do an inspection together shortly, but for now, relax and enjoy your breakfast while I make a few phone calls to tie up some administrative loose ends."

As Warden Brown busies himself on the phone, Toby sips his coffee quietly. Though he can hear the conversation, he doesn't grasp its context. Unbeknownst to him, the pleasant start to the day is about to take a dark turn, one he could never have anticipated. Warden Brown's smiles and cheerful demeanour are a façade, masking a calculating, untrustworthy man with a blemished record of deception and corruption. He is in league with the notorious Quad: Governor Boris, Governess Olga, and Judge Edward-Vernon-Blake. A changing of the guard is imminent, and the truth will soon surface.

The calm ambiance shatters abruptly. Gunshots ring out in rapid succession.

"What on earth is that noise?" Toby exclaims. "It sounds like fireworks!"

"Let's take a look," Warden Brown says calmly. "Follow me to the window, Toby."

A chilling flashback hits Toby like a brick. The last time he was led to this window, upon his arrival at Pentridge, the Warden had pointed to the prison cemetery and said, *"That's where you're going to be buried."* Hesitantly, Toby approaches the window with the Warden and gasps.

"It's not fireworks!" he cries. "It's gunfire, people are being shot!"

"Indeed," the Warden replies coolly. "Take a closer look, Toby. Recognize the clothing?"

Toby's heart sinks. "Those men are wearing black cloaks, aren't they?"

"Correct," the Warden says, a smirk in his voice.

Toby's face turns pale, and he freezes. "My monks!" he yells. "My monks have just been shot!"

"Yes, indeed," the Warden confirms. "They were vermin, Toby, nasty criminals, the scum of society. They had to be eliminated, eradicated from the face of the earth. My phone call earlier was about cleansing society of such filth. It's my duty."

Toby is reeling, but the Warden presses on. "Let's go inspect your workshop to confirm its readiness."

They exit the office and head toward the lift. Toby, still shaken, has been in this lift before. After exiting, the Warden turns right instead of left.

"Warden, I think you're going the wrong way," Toby says. "The workshop is to the left."

The Warden's reply is sharp. "That can wait. You're coming with me."

An electronic door opens, and suddenly, Toby finds himself in the prison graveyard. Fear floods his face.

"Let's take a stroll, shall we?" the Warden says mockingly.

As they walk along a cobblestone path, Toby sees the monks' lifeless bodies, dressed in black robes, laid beside empty burial plots. To his right, prisoners with shovels stand ready to dig. Toby begins to sob.

"There, there," the Warden says dismissively. "We haven't finished the tour yet."

More gunshots ring out nearby, followed by silence.

"Now we can continue," the Warden says.

Further down the path, Toby spots another row of bodies. As he draws closer, he cries out, "No! They're my truck drivers!"

"Correct again, Toby," the Warden says, his tone mocking. "You're earning a gold star today. Same story, different criminals. It's an eradication program. The vermin must be made extinct, banished from the earth. It warms my heart to see my work done."

Toby slumps to the ground, sobbing.

"Don't worry, Toby," the Warden says. "Nothing like that will happen to you. Let's head back to my office for another coffee. I have good news, I promise, you'll love it."

Toby rises, head bowed, deeply troubled. The Warden glances at him, shakes his head, but says nothing. He pulls out his phone. "Yes, can I have a fresh pot of coffee delivered to my office in a few minutes?"

Back in the office, the coffee arrives. "Come on, Toby, brighten up," the Warden says. "This is all in a day's work. Pour yourself a cup, my news will cheer you up. Your wife is coming to see you today!"

Toby's face lights up.

"And that's not all," the Warden continues. "Your mate Augustus is coming too."

"Wow!" Toby shouts. "That's the best news ever! I'm so excited to see my wife and Augustus. It's been so long."

"I told you it would cheer you up," the Warden says. "Now relax, sip your coffee, and then we'll head to the workshop to ensure everything's on track."

As Toby relaxes in a winged-back chair, the office phone rings. The Warden answers. "Hello, Edward! Great to hear from you. What's on your mind this fine morning?"

It's Judge Edward-Vernon-Blake. "Are you alone?" he asks.

"No, Judge, Toby's here. We're discussing last-minute preparations for the workshop."

"Get rid of him. I need to talk."

"Hold on, Judge," the Warden says. "Toby, there's a delivery at the loading dock near the workshop. Can you go accept it?"

"Sure," Toby replies, leaving immediately.

"Hi, Edward, he's gone," the Warden says. "We can talk freely now."

"There's a cupboard to your right with straightjackets on a shelf," the Judge instructs. "Take the box of straightjackets and place them behind the workshop stage. I'll fill you in when I arrive later. What's been happening this morning, Warden?"

"Oh, it's been productive," the Warden replies. "I organized the firing squad to take out the monks and truck drivers, as you requested. It was amazing to watch. Toby was here when the shooting started and thought it was fireworks. I took him to the window to see the monks being shot, his face went pale with fright. I had to look away to keep from laughing. Then I took him to the graveyard. He saw the monks' bodies, fell to his knees, and cried. Later, he saw the truck drivers' bodies and sobbed again. Your orders have been carried out, Judge."

"Great work, Warden," the Judge says. "You'll be rewarded for your magnificent efforts."

"Thank you, Judge," the Warden replies. "It was a pleasure. I must go now, Toby's waiting at the workshop for the delivery. We'll talk more when you arrive."

At the workshop, the foundational HTML Warden Brown arrives and finds Toby. "Hey, Toby, how's it going?"

"All good, Warden," Toby replies. "I've signed for the delivery and placed the boxes in the corner on the stage."

"Well done, Toby," the Warden says, opening a box to find curtains. "That reminds me, I must call the curtain company to install them."

Soon, a team arrives to set up electronic curtains that slide open and closed across the stage, reminiscent of those at a cremation service, signalling the final chapter of a life, a morbid but undeniable truth.

Toby gives the Warden a tour of the workshop, a massive structure capable of housing over a thousand people. Divided into sections with partitions, decorated with palm trees and pot plants, and equipped with kitchens and coffee stations, it's a first-class facility. The Warden is impressed by Toby's layout, which includes fully functional workstations for metalwork, woodworking, and art, among others. Toby has assigned prisoners to their chosen activities, with specialists ready to guide them.

"Impressive, Toby," the Warden says. "You've done an amazing job. I'll ensure something special happens for you today, a surprise for everyone."

The Warden glances at the stage, where the curtains are being tested. His thoughts drift to last week's Quad meeting with Governor Boris, Governess Olga, Judge Edward-Vernon-Blake, and himself, where they devised a sinister plan, a meticulously crafted scheme with disastrous consequences for a chosen trio. *We are The Quad, The Quad Rising. A new empire will rise.*

A consultant interrupts, offering to demonstrate the curtain remote. The Warden tests its functions, pause, fast, slow, delighted by the control.

"Thank you, you've done an amazing job," he tells the team.

He closes the curtains completely, needing to distract Toby to set up items on the stage. He calls Officer Rodney. "I need you to gather officers and meet me at the workshop ASAP."

When they arrive, the Warden explains, "First, I need a distraction for Toby. Officer Stevens, take him out of the building so I can prepare a special surprise."

Toby is introduced to Officer Stevens. "I told you something special would happen today," the Warden says. "Stevens is taking you out for coffee and cake. Discuss your plans for today's events, take your time, and enjoy. This is your reward, Toby."

With Toby gone, the Warden instructs his officers. "In the storeroom, there are treasure chests to be placed on the stage. Set three chairs in front of them, evenly spaced. Don't ask questions, just do it."

The officers comply, and the Warden retrieves the box of straightjackets from behind the stage, placing one under each chair as per the Judge's orders. Suddenly, Judge Edward-Vernon-Blake appears, startling him.

"Sorry, Warden, I didn't mean to scare you," the Judge says. "I arrived early, too excited for today. Olga will join us soon to review our plan. Boris is on his way, traffic permitting."

The Quad assembles on stage, admiring the treasure chests and straightjackets. "Well done, Warden," the Judge says. "You've earned your place in The Quad. Can we speak freely?"

"Yes, Judge," the Warden replies. "Toby is gone. We're alone."

In a jest, the Warden says, "Ready to try on the straightjackets under your seats?"

Laughter erupts. "Very funny, Warden," the trio says. "Maybe you should do a comedy act today."

The Judge glances at the ceiling. "I assume you've arranged the space up there for, you know, what's to happen?"

"Yes, Judge," the Warden confirms. "It's taken care of, and the team is ready."

The Judge smiles and winks.

At Farnworth Detention Centre, twenty-five coaches and a special disabled taxi for Augustus arrive, organized by Governor Boris. Handcuffed and shackled prisoners are loaded onto the coaches with extra officers ensuring a smooth process. Augustus, frail and confused, is wheeled out in his wheelchair, unaware of his destination. Once in the taxi, an officer reveals, "You're going to see your mate Toby at Pentridge's new workshop."

Augustus smiles. "I can't believe I'm seeing Toby after so long. I never knew where he was sent after we were split up."

"You'll have plenty to talk about," the officer says. "And there's another surprise. You're seeing another friend today, Marguerite."

Augustus is stunned. "You're kidding! Marguerite? And all the women from Barwon Prison Facility are coming too?"

"Yes," the officer confirms. "It's a new integration initiative, men and women prisoners meeting weekly. Today's the trial. Forget revenge, Augustus. Focus on reuniting with your friends."

"I guess you're right," Augustus says. "With my time running out, I should enjoy these moments."

At Barwon Prison Facility for Women, twenty-five coaches arrive to transport the women to Pentridge. Handcuffed and shackled, they're logged and seated with meticulous care to prevent escapes. Governess Olga has emphasized maximum security, warning that any mistakes will cost jobs.

As the women board, excitement mounts, perhaps at the prospect of seeing men. Nina, a known prankster, jokes, "I might propose to a fella at Pentridge. That'll mess up your integration program. Ever thought about married prisoners sharing cells?"

The officer chuckles. "Well said, Nina. I'll pass it on. But keep the flirting minimal, Governess Olga is watching, and there'll be consequences for misbehaviour."

The coaches arrive at Pentridge's workshop. Toby greets over seven hundred guests, ushering them to their designated seats and work areas. Meanwhile, Augustus and Marguerite are escorted through a back entrance behind the stage, where The Quad awaits.

"Oh, no!" Augustus bellows. "Not you lot! I wouldn't have come if I'd known."

Marguerite, mute after having her tongue cut out, shows shock through her frail expression. They're seated at a round table near the stage with The Quad and two officers. Toby, busy with guests, is unaware of their presence but will soon notice as he nears the stage.

Governess Olga pulls a sign from her handbag and taunts Marguerite. "I've got a present for you, dear." She shoves the sign in Marguerite's face, which reads, *"I can't talk, they cut my tongue out!"* Tears stream down Marguerite's face.

"Oh, what's the matter, dear? Cat got your tongue?" Olga sneers.

"You bitch!" Augustus snaps, despite his restraints. He leans over, reads the sign, and gasps. Olga hangs it around Marguerite's neck for all to see.

Marguerite notices Augustus's wheelchair and missing legs. "They chopped my legs off with a circular saw," he says bitterly.

Marguerite bows her head, sobbing quietly. The shock overwhelms them both.

Toby, nearing the stage, spots Marguerite and the sign. He freezes, barely recognizing her sunken, toothless face. She holds up the sign, and Toby's heart breaks. Warden Brown pulls out a chair. "Sit," he orders.

Toby glares at Marguerite, then at Augustus. "My goodness, you've got no legs! What happened?"

Overwhelmed, Toby sobs into his hands. The Quad show no sympathy. "Shut up and stop blubbering," they snap. "They deserved it, and you'll get yours if you don't quiet down. Speeches are starting."

Warden Brown steps to the microphone. "Welcome, everyone. This is the new dawn of prison management, integration begins now. Familiarize yourselves with your chosen projects in this magnificent space, built for both men and women to collaborate without prejudice. I hope you feel welcome."

He introduces Judge Edward-Vernon-Blake, who steps to the microphone but pauses, whispering to the officers. Marguerite, Augustus, and Toby are escorted around the corner. The Warden slips the curtain remote into the Judge's pocket and confirms, "The snipers are in position."

The Judge returns to the microphone. "I'm pleased to welcome you all to this wonderful venue. From time to time, we reflect on events that changed the world, and closer to home, those that affected us. I speak of loved ones lost to the murderous rampage of a few, the masterminds who built an empire of wealth but destroyed innocent lives. I'm talking about that trio."

He presses the remote. The curtains open, revealing Toby, Augustus, and Marguerite in straightjackets.

"I'm talking about *this* trio," the Judge declares. "I had the pleasure of incarcerating them for their heinous crimes against humanity, against *you* and your loved ones. They're worthy of restraint. The treasure chests on stage held the money they stole. Their mansion has been sold. Atrocities happened there at their hands. I should've listened to public opinion, they'd have said, 'They should be shot!'"

Gunfire erupts. The trio falls, shot dead. The curtains close.

Their Final Curtain Call

The Trio is Dead.

Memoriam

The community gathers at the Town Square,
 Consumed by grief and loss.
 We pay homage to the fallen, our loved ones.
 Taken far too soon under terrible circumstances.

We remember the love they gave us;
 They remain forever in our hearts and thoughts.
 Bless their souls.
 Though departed, they are never forgotten.

Let us join hands and pray:
 Lord, hear our prayers.
 Grant us the strength to forgive and move forward.
 May our loved one's rest in eternal peace.

We, left in tatters and heartbreak,
 Will heal, in time.

The perpetrators,
 They are dead.
 They now burn in Hell,
 An eternity of fire
 You so richly deserve.

Glyn Lewis Author:

Melbourne Australia

I sincerely hope that you enjoy this Psychological Thriller.

I am currently working on a sequel to

The Dead see Everything

It is currently in production

I would like to make mention my gratitude to my Publisher

Inkwavespublishing.com

Special thanks to Samual and Jason

The Writers and Publishing Teams

The Art department for an Amazing Cover.

Thank you for your communication during this project You are all Outstanding.

The Quad Rising
The Sequel to
The Dead see Everything
By
Glyn Lewis

THE BRIDE OF FIRE

GLYN LEWIS

THE BRIDE OF FIRE

Meet Chantelle Franks: Ambitious, unstoppable, and dangerous.

New York City has met its match in Chantelle Franks, a brilliant divorce lawyer with a sharp mind and an even sharper edge. With a Harvard degree and a chilling disregard for boundaries, Chantelle's path to success is paved with meticulous planning and an unflinching willingness to eliminate obstacles—no matter the cost.

Her lover is a pawn in her grand design, her enemies mere stepping stones, and her own mother a target of her unrelenting scorn. Chantelle thrives in a world of power and control, but the deeper she delves into manipulation and vengeance, the more precarious her empire becomes. Powerful, gripping, and twisted, Chantelle Franks: The Price of Control is a psychological thriller that will leave you questioning how far one woman will go to claim her place at the top.

Powerful, gripping, and twisted, Chantelle Franks: The Price of Control is a psychological thriller that will leave you questioning how far one woman will go to claim her place at the top.

GLYN LEWIS

ISBN 9798305000429

90000

9 798305 000429

2/21/25 4:53 PM

Mr Barky B

Loves his Lemon Tree

By Glyn Lewis

Discover the Magic of Reading Under the Lemon Tree!

Join Mr. Barky B, the joyful and ever enthusiastic dog, on an enchanting journey beneath the vibrant Lemon Tree.

With his best friend Penny Puppy by his side, Mr. Barky inspires children to embrace the joy of books, transforming reading into a delightful adventure.

From guiding a lost toad back home with the power of words to helping a curious bear explore new worlds, Mr. Barky B shows how reading unlocks limitless possibilities.

Along the way, he's joined by Colin the Clown and a host of lovable characters, each discovering the wonder and empowerment that comes with learning to read.

This heartwarming story is not just about letters and words—it's about friendship, imagination, and the magic of opening doors to new adventures. Perfect for young readers, Mr. Barky B Loves His Lemon Tree will leave children smiling and inspired to read under their very own lemon tree.

Glyn Lewis
Melbourne Australia.

Glyn's Book Store

Inquiries:
glynyes@gmail.com

Glyn's Website

www.ingramcontent.com/pod-product-compliance
Lightning Source LLC
Chambersburg PA
CBHW080953120626
46546CB00010B/2882